THE OFFICIAL COOKBOOK

OVERWATCH®

THE OFFICIAL COOKBOOK

CHELSEA MONROE-CASSEL

INSIGHT
EDITIONS

San Rafael, California

CONTENTS

INTRODUCTION

Welcome to the Overwatch kitchen, agent!

The heroes of Overwatch might be divided at times by their goals and organizations, but one thing that always brings everyone together is a love of good food. This cookbook will explore some of our heroes' favorite recipes from their homelands and the new foods they have discovered on their travels.

These recipes are organized geographically and by character so you can explore the cultural similarities and differences among the heroes of Overwatch and among different regions of the world. While I've striven to be as authentic as possible, I deviate slightly from tradition on some recipes to make them more approachable.

One of the trickiest aspects of international cooking can be finding regional ingredients, but that can also be a fun adventure! Small local markets will often yield the ingredients you need, along with other surprising finds like a new fruit or snack you've never seen before. If all else fails, online shopping can usually supply you with whatever you might need. Feel free to embrace your inner scientist or engineer and tweak these recipes depending on your dietary needs and the ingredients available to you.

Above all, this collection is a great way to discover new cuisines and learn about food cultures around the world! Talon might believe that humanity evolves only through conflict, but the heroes of Overwatch know that a plate of good food made with care might be just what we all need to come together.

Are you with me?

—Chelsea Monroe-Cassel

THE AMERICAS

CARNE ADOVADA

A tender pork dish bursting with flavors and desert spice, carne adovada is a classic Southwest favorite. This recipe tastes even better the next day, and the level of heat can be adjusted to preference.

Jesse McCree found this particular version being made in a hole-in-the-wall place on Route 66, just outside Albuquerque, New Mexico. Although his work with Blackwatch took him across the world, he always made sure to stop back in for a hearty serving whenever he was in town.

THE AMERICAS • McCree

TYPE: **COMFORT**

PREP TIME: 30 minutes
COOKING TIME: 2 hours

YIELD: 8 servings

DIETARY: Gluten-Free

- » ⅓ cup vegetable oil
- » 1 yellow onion, diced
- » 3 to 4 cloves garlic, minced
- » 2½ pounds pork loin, cut into bite-size cubes
- » 4 cups chicken stock, divided
- » 2 teaspoons ground coriander seed
- » 2 teaspoons dried Mexican oregano
- » 2 tablespoons red chili powder
- » 1 teaspoon ground cinnamon
- » 1 teaspoon ground cumin
- » 1 tablespoon honey
- » 2 tablespoons red wine vinegar
- » Salt, to taste

1. Preheat the oven to 350°F and set aside a Dutch oven or large casserole dish.

2. In a large frying pan, heat the oil over medium heat. Add the onion and garlic, and cook for a few minutes, until both are soft and golden brown. Transfer the onion and garlic to the bowl of a food processor or blender. Next, brown the pork on all sides in the same frying pan in batches. Add a little more oil to the pan if needed. When all the pork is browned, transfer it to the Dutch oven.

3. Blend the onion, garlic, 1 cup of chicken stock, spices, honey, and vinegar until smooth, then pour over the pork in the Dutch oven. Add the remaining chicken stock until all the pork is submerged. Cook uncovered for around 2 hours, until the pork is very tender and the sauce has thickened somewhat. Add salt to taste and serve. This recipe is great served over rice.

"Not bad, if I do say so myself."

BISCOCHITOS

A longtime resident of the Southwest, where cultures collide and outlaw justice prevails, Jesse McCree built his own personal brand of right and wrong. Also born out of complex history, these cookies have a decidedly old-world flavor with a twist, as savory fat balances out the sweetness, and robust spices complement the whole. Plates of these treats are often found gracing tables in the Southwest during holidays and other special occasions.

McCree may look like a no-nonsense cowboy, but a traditional cookie from home is just the thing to crack his veneer. Even outlaws need to celebrate every now and then. Plus, keeping up the fight for justice definitely merits a cookie break.

 PREP TIME: 10 minutes
CHILLING TIME: 30 minutes
BAKING TIME: 10 minutes

 *YIELD:* About 2 dozen cookies

 *DIETARY:* None

COOKIES

- ½ cup lard
- ¼ cup unsalted butter, softened
- ¼ cup sugar
- 1½ teaspoons baking powder
- 1 egg
- ½ teaspoon vanilla extract
- Zest of one orange
- Pinch of salt
- 2 teaspoons crushed anise seed
- 1½ cups all-purpose flour

TOPPINGS

- ½ cup sugar
- 1 teaspoon ground cinnamon

1. In a medium-size mixing bowl, cream together the lard, butter, sugar, and baking powder. Add the egg and vanilla, followed by the orange zest, salt, and anise seed. Stir in the flour until you have a soft dough that holds together. Wrap in plastic and chill for 30 minutes.

2. When you are ready to bake, preheat the oven to 350°F and line a baking sheet with parchment paper. Combine the sugar and cinnamon in a small bowl and set to one side.

3. Roll out the chilled dough on a lightly floured surface to about ¼ inch thick. Use a cookie cutter or a knife to cut into your desired shape and place the cookies on the prepared baking sheet. Bake for about 10 minutes or until slightly golden. Let the cookies cool for a few minutes; then, working with one cookie at a time, coat the cookies in the cinnamon-sugar mixture before setting on a wire rack to finish cooling.

"Back into the mix."

DEADEYE

While a steaming pot of black piñon coffee will get the gears going on an early-morning mission, sometimes Jesse McCree prefers a drink with a little more bite. Made at the notorious Calaveras bar, this cocktail featuring black tea and bourbon goes down smooth and hits like a flashbang.

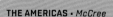

THE AMERICAS • *McCree*

TYPE: *DRINK*

PREP TIME: 5 minutes
CHILLING TIME: 1 hour

YIELD: 2 servings

DIETARY: Gluten-Free, Vegetarian

» 2 cups boiling water
» ½ cup sugar
» 4 black tea bags
» 4 ounces bourbon, divided
» Ice
» Lemon and mint to garnish

1. Combine the water, sugar, and tea bags in a heatproof medium-size mixing bowl or pitcher. Stir the water until the sugar has dissolved completely, and then let the mixture steep for 5 minutes.

2. Take out the tea bags and chill the tea mixture for around an hour, or until cold. Mix half the tea mixture with 2 ounces bourbon, and then pour over ice in a lowball glass. Garnish with lemon and mint.

"Next round's on me."

CORN PUDDING

Though it's labeled a pudding, this delicious recipe is no dessert. Full of bite and savory flavor, each tender spoonful is both satisfying and deeply comforting.

Ashe's butler, Bob, used to make this for her when she was a small girl, often when her parents were out of town on business. Even now, without being asked, he can quickly whip up a steaming bowl of this pudding after a heist gone sideways or the sudden reappearance of a troublesome acquaintance.

TYPE: *COMFORT*

 PREP TIME: 10 minutes
COOKING TIME: 30 minutes

 YIELD: 6 to 8 servings

 DIETARY: Vegetarian

- 4 eggs
- 1½ cups heavy cream
- ¼ cup unsalted butter, melted
- ¼ cup sugar
- 2 teaspoons baking powder
- 1½ teaspoons salt
- 3 tablespoons all-purpose flour
- ½ teaspoon thyme
- ¼ teaspoon cumin
- ½ teaspoon crushed red pepper
- 1 cup shredded cheddar cheese
- 6 cups corn kernels (about 1½ pounds)

1. Preheat the oven to 350°F and lightly butter a large casserole dish.

2. Whisk together the eggs, cream, and melted butter in a large mixing bowl. Add the sugar, baking powder, salt, flour, and seasonings, beating until completely mixed. Switch to a mixing spoon and add the cheese, followed by the corn kernels. Transfer everything over to the prepared casserole dish, and then bake for around 30 minutes, or until the pudding has set and is a nice golden brown on top.

TIP: This recipe can also be baked in individual ramekins but will require less time in the oven.

"That's rich."

ORANGE CRÈME CARAMEL

While a lot of folks think flan is a daunting undertaking, this recipe is far from difficult. With a little patience, the reward of a sweet, melt-in-your-mouth flan with subtle orange flavor is better than any bounty. A lot of desserts have been spoiled for Ashe by the memory of bad birthdays and neglected holidays, but this one remains one of her very favorites.

THE AMERICAS · *Ashe*

TYPE: *CELEBRATORY*

 PREP TIME: 25 minutes
BAKING TIME: 25 to 30 minutes
CHILLING TIME: 2 hours 15 minutes minimum

 YIELD: 4 good-size flans

DIETARY: Gluten-Free, Vegetarian

» 1 cup granulated sugar

» 2 tablespoons room-temperature water

» 1 drop of lemon juice

» Unsalted butter, for greasing the ramekins

» One 14-ounce can sweetened condensed milk

» ½ cup freshly squeezed orange juice

» ¼ cup half-and-half or whole milk

» 5 large eggs

» ¼ cup orange liqueur

» Berries to garnish

1. Set out four medium-size ramekins near your stovetop.

2. Combine the sugar, water, and drop of lemon juice in a medium saucepan over medium-low heat. Stir until the sugar dissolves, and then stop stirring. Continue to cook until the mixture thickens a bit and turns a nice light amber color, and then remove from heat and pour into your ramekins. Tilt the ramekins to be sure the caramel coats the bottoms of the dishes. Set these aside to cool completely.

3. Once the caramel has cooled in the ramekins, preheat the oven to 325°F. Butter the sides of the ramekins above the caramel layer, and then set the ramekins in a baking dish with tall sides. In a medium-size bowl, thoroughly beat together the remaining ingredients, scraping the bottom of the bowl to be sure nothing has settled.

4. Pour the mixture into the ramekins, making sure to distribute the flan evenly between the ramekins. Pour boiling water into the baking dish so it covers up to about the halfway point on the ramekins, and then move the tray to the oven.

5. Bake for around 25 to 30 minutes, until the flan is set around the edges but still has some wobble in the middle. Remove from the oven and set the flans on a cooling rack for around 15 minutes, then pop them in the fridge for at least 2 hours. Letting the flan sit overnight is better, to allow the caramel to blend with the flan and for the sides to pull away from the ramekin slightly.

6. When you're ready to serve, run a sharp knife around the edge of the flan to help release it from the ramekin. Set the bottom of each ramekin into a bowl with a little boiling water to help heat the caramel layer back up. Remove the ramekins from the water, and then place a serving plate upside down on top of the ramekin (the top of the plate should be against the ramekin mouth). Then, holding them tightly together, flip the plate and ramekin around so the plate is facing up with the ramekin inverted atop it. Give them both a few good shakes up and down (listen for the sound of the flan releasing), and then gently lift off the ramekin. The flan should be plated successfully, with a pool of caramel swirling around it. Serve straightaway, garnished with berries, if you like.

"You haven't seen anything yet."

TEXAS FIZZ

A little self-care after a long day of running a gang of misfits and rebels helps Ashe unwind and hit the ground running for the next challenge. She might be the calculating leader of the Deadlock Gang, but even she enjoys the occasional fizzy, refreshing beverage. After all, her business, her rules.

THE AMERICAS · *Ashe*

TYPE: *DRINK*

 PREP TIME: 5 minutes

 YIELD: 1 serving

 DIETARY: Gluten-Free, Vegetarian

» 1½ ounces gin
» 1 ounce orange juice
» ½ ounce grenadine or more to taste
» 2 to 3 ounces champagne
» Ice

1. Combine the gin, orange juice, and grenadine in a shaker half filled with ice. Shake for several seconds to combine, and then pour into a flute glass.

2. Top up with champagne and serve immediately.

"It's all about life's little pleasures."

BUTTERMILK FLAPJACKS

Few homemade breakfasts can compare with the satisfaction and speed of pancakes. In just a few minutes, you'll have a towering stack of delicious flapjacks dripping with syrup that disappear just as quickly as they appeared.

    Back before Overwatch's collapse, Jack Morrison was known to whip up a quick stack of flapjacks for breakfast with Ana Amari, adding a pinch of cinnamon and a bit of orange zest to the batter. He swore the orange flavor gave the pancakes a little extra pick-me-up first thing in the morning—perfect for meeting a mission head-on.

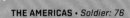

THE AMERICAS · *Soldier: 76*

TYPE: *PREP*

 PREP TIME: 5 minutes
COOKING: 15 minutes minimum, depending on the size of the pan or griddle

 YIELD: A dozen small pancakes or 4 to 6 large ones

 DIETARY: Vegetarian

PANCAKES:

» 1½ cups buttermilk, room temperature

» 6 tablespoons unsalted butter, melted

» 2 eggs

» 4 tablespoons sugar

» 2 cups all-purpose flour, divided

» 2 teaspoons baking powder

» ½ teaspoon salt

» Zest of one orange (optional)

» 1 teaspoon ground cinnamon (optional)

TOPPINGS:

» Blueberries

» Strawberries

» Whipped cream

» Butter

» Maple syrup

1. In a mixing bowl, whisk together the buttermilk, butter, eggs, and sugar. Add half the flour, followed by the baking powder and salt. Add the orange zest and cinnamon, if using. Gradually whisk in the rest of the flour until you have a nice smooth batter that drops easily from a spoon; you may need to add a little extra flour or buttermilk, depending on the size of your eggs.

2. Preheat a pan or griddle over medium-low heat. The pan is ready when a drop of water sprinkled on the pan's surface sizzles and dances.

3. When the pan is hot, drop the batter onto it: For small pancakes, spoon a couple of tablespoons onto the pan at a time, and for larger pancakes, spoon about ⅓ cup at a time. Let the pancakes cook for about a minute and a half on the first side until the batter in the middle of the pancakes stops bubbling and begins to set. Carefully flip over the pancakes and cook for another minute or so, until both sides are a lovely golden brown.

4. Serve warm, topped with butter, fresh berries, and whipped cream and drizzled liberally with maple syrup.

"You want flapjacks done right, you've got to do it yourself."

TATER TOT HOT DISH

Like its old-world cousin, this Midwestern take on shepherd's pie is comfort food at its best. The concept is straightforward: meat and vegetables in a flavorful gravy topped with crispy tater tots. This warming recipe was a staple in the Morrison family meal rotation, usually right between meatloaf night and chicken-and-biscuits Sunday. Jack still makes this recipe on nights when he is feeling particularly wistful. Its flexibility allows him to use whatever meat or vegetables he has on hand—a good soldier knows better than to waste resources.

THE AMERICAS · *Soldier: 76*

TYPE: COMFORT

 **PREP TIME:** 15 minutes
BAKING TIME: 35 minutes

 **YIELD:** 4 to 6 servings

 **DIETARY:** Gluten-Free

- » 2 tablespoons olive oil
- » 2 cloves garlic, minced
- » 1½ pounds ground beef
- » ¼ cup packed dark brown sugar
- » 2 tablespoons tomato paste
- » 1 tablespoon Worcestershire sauce
- » ½ teaspoon dried savory
- » 1 cup mixed frozen vegetables
- » Salt and pepper, to taste
- » 1½ cups shredded cheddar cheese
- » One 32-ounce bag of frozen tater tots

1. Preheat the oven to 425°F and set out an 8-by-11-inch casserole dish.

2. Heat the olive oil in a large frying pan over medium heat. Cook the garlic for several minutes, until golden brown and fragrant. Add the ground beef to the pan and cook another few minutes, breaking up, until completely browned. Stir in the brown sugar, tomato paste, Worcestershire sauce, savory, and vegetables. Stir to combine completely, then add salt and pepper to taste. Remove from heat and transfer the mixture to the readied casserole dish.

3. Top the meat mixture evenly with the shredded cheese, and then carefully lay out the frozen tater tots on top in even rows. Move to the oven and bake for 30 minutes or until tater tots are crispy. To make the top extra crispy, you can pop the dish under the broiler for another few minutes, but keep a close eye on it to make sure it doesn't burn. Serve hot with ketchup or other condiments of your choice.

"That's 'chef,' to you."

HOOSIER SUGAR CREAM PIE

Midwesterners have to get a little creative during the winter months when fresh fruit isn't readily available, and there's no better solution than Indiana's state pie. This comforting and creamy pie can be made year-round and tastes like eggnog. A slice of Hoosier sugar cream pie was one food Jack loved to share with his former boyfriend, Vincent, on the rare peaceful weekend.

THE AMERICAS • *Soldier: 76*

TYPE: *CELEBRATORY*

PREP TIME: 1 hour 15 minutes
BAKING TIME: 25 minutes

YIELD: 1 pie, at least 8 servings

DIETARY: Vegetarian

CRUST:

» 1¼ cups all-purpose flour
» 1 tablespoon sugar
» Pinch of salt
» 6 tablespoons unsalted butter
» ⅓ cup ice water

FILLING:

» 1½ cups whole milk
» 1½ cups heavy cream
» 1 cup granulated sugar
» ¼ teaspoon nutmeg
» ¼ cup cornstarch
» Pinch of salt
» 1 teaspoon vanilla extract
» 2 tablespoons unsalted butter
» Cinnamon and nutmeg, for sprinkling

TO MAKE THE CRUST:

1. In a small mixing bowl, combine the flour, sugar, and salt. Rub in the butter until the texture resembles coarse breadcrumbs. Add the ice water a bit at a time, as you continue mixing until the dough just starts to come together—you may not use all the water. Roll the dough into a ball and wrap in plastic wrap, and then let chill for at least an hour.

TO MAKE THE FILLING:

2. In a medium saucepan, whisk together the milk, cream, sugar, nutmeg, cornstarch, and salt. Bring the mixture to a simmer, whisking constantly to make sure it doesn't stick to the bottom of the pan. Cook for about 10 minutes, or until the mixture has thickened considerably and is bubbling. Remove from heat and whisk in the vanilla and butter. Set this mixture aside.

3. Preheat the oven to 375°F. Roll out the chilled dough and drape over a lightly buttered pie pan. Trim off any excess, and press and decorate the edges however you please. Prick the pastry all over with a fork to keep it from bubbling up. Bake for about 10 minutes, until just light brown. Pour the prepared filling into the lightly baked shell. Return to oven and bake for another 15 minutes until it is bubbling slightly around the edges. Remove from oven and let cool overnight or at least 8 hours to be sure it's completely set. Just before serving, sprinkle with a light dusting of cinnamon and nutmeg. This pie can be served rewarmed or chilled.

"I could do this with my eyes closed."

THE 76

Nothing says summertime like a good ice-cold milkshake! Summer evenings were hot in Bloomington, Indiana, where Jack grew up. But after a long day of working on the farm, he was free to go spend time with friends at the local ice cream shop, where this milkshake was a specialty.

THE AMERICAS · *Soldier: 76*

TYPE: *DRINK*

 PREP TIME: 15 minutes

 YIELD: 2 servings

 **DIETARY:** Gluten-Free, Vegetarian

» 1½ cups heavy cream, divided

» 1 cup white chocolate chips

» Red, white, and blue sprinkles

» Red food coloring

» Blue food coloring

» 2 cups whole milk

» 8 scoops of vanilla ice cream

» 1 teaspoon vanilla extract

1. Start by combining ½ cup of the heavy cream and all the white chocolate in a small bowl. Microwave in 20-second bursts, being sure to stir in between each burst, until the chocolate is melted. Dip the rims of two tall serving glasses in the white chocolate, let any excess drip off, and then roll in the red, white, and blue sprinkles to make a festive rim.

2. Mix the red food coloring with the remaining chocolate until you have a nice bright color. Using a spoon or a piping bag, drizzle stripes of red down the inside of the glass. Set aside or in the freezer to chill.

3. Make the whipped cream by beating the remaining 1 cup of heavy cream with an electric mixer until stiff peaks form, which should take only a minute or two. Beat in the blue food coloring, and then set the whipped cream aside.

4. Combine the milk, ice cream, and vanilla extract in a blender and blend until smooth. Pour the milkshake into the prepared glasses, top with blue whipped cream, and serve with straws.

TIP: You can use different colors of food coloring and sprinkles to support your favorite *Overwatch* League team!

"Stay frosty."

BREAKFAST QUESADILLA

This breakfast quesadilla was one of Gabriel Reyes's go-to meals while growing up in Los Angeles for its easy assembly and high protein content. Just like a Blackwatch strike team, this breakfast dish is readily adaptable; while this recipe starts off vegetarian, Reyes was known to add his favorite chorizo to mix things up. Feel free to add some salsas and other dipping sauces when serving.

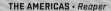

THE AMERICAS • *Reaper*

TYPE: *PREP*

 PREP TIME: 5 minutes
COOKING TIME: 10 minutes

 YIELD: 1 quesadilla

 DIETARY: Vegetarian

» 2 eggs
» Hot sauce
» Pinch of salt
» Pinch of pepper
» ½ cup canned black beans, rinsed and drained
» 2 tablespoons unsalted butter
» Two 8-inch flour tortillas
» ½ cup grated cheddar cheese, divided
» ½ avocado, diced
» 1 tablespoon chopped green onion
» 1 tablespoon finely chopped cilantro

1. Beat the eggs with the hot sauce to taste, salt, and pepper in a small bowl, and then add the beans.

2. Melt the butter in a frying pan over medium heat, and then add the egg mixture and cook, stirring constantly for a couple of minutes, until the eggs are just cooked but not hard. Transfer the cooked eggs into a clean bowl.

3. In a clean frying pan, heat one of the tortillas over medium heat. Spread it with half of the cheese and let the tortilla cook in the pan until the cheese has melted.

4. Spread the cooked eggs evenly over the cheese, and then sprinkle on a layer of avocado, green onion, and cilantro. Sprinkle the rest of the cheese on top of the quesadilla, and then place the second tortilla on top, pressing down slightly.

5. Reduce the heat in the pan a little and cook the quesadilla on both sides for a minute or so, until golden and crispy. Transfer the quesadilla to a cutting board and chop into triangles.

TIP: This is a very flexible recipe, once you get the hang of it. Experiment with adding your favorite breakfast sausage or different types of beans and cheeses.

"It's in the refrigerator."

CHILI CON QUESO

Chili con queso is a warm and savory Tex-Mex dish that is quite a crowd-pleaser when served as an appetizer with tortilla chips. While much has changed for Reyes since undergoing Moira's extensive experiments, a bowl of queso on a rough day still warms his dark heart.

THE AMERICAS • Reaper

TYPE: *COMFORT*

PREP TIME: 5 minutes
COOKING TIME: 20 minutes

YIELD: 1 party-size serving for 6 to 8 people

DIETARY: Vegetarian

- 3 tablespoons unsalted butter
- 1 small yellow onion, diced
- 1 jalapeño pepper, seeded and diced
- 4 cloves garlic, minced
- 3 tablespoons all-purpose flour
- 1 cup whole milk
- 1 cup heavy cream
- ¼ teaspoon cumin
- ¼ teaspoon salt
- 4 ounces grated sharp cheddar cheese
- 4 ounces grated pepper jack cheese
- ⅓ cup fire-roasted diced tomatoes

1. Melt the butter in a medium saucepan over medium heat. Add the onion, jalapeño, and garlic. Cook for 5 to 10 minutes, until the onions are soft and the mix is fragrant. Sprinkle in the flour and stir until the flour is completely absorbed by the butter.

2. Gradually pour in the milk and heavy cream while whisking until you have a nice thickened mixture.

3. Remove from heat and stir in the cumin and salt, followed by the cheeses. Finally, stir in the tomatoes. Serve warm with tortilla chips.

"The darkness consumes."

CHURROS WITH CAJETA

Though it's hard to imagine it now, a younger Gabriel Reyes once enjoyed sitting down to share a plate of these churros with his former Overwatch teammates Jack Morrison and Ana Amari after a successful mission.

These sweet lengths of fried dough are true delights, with a crunchy sweet exterior and a soft, doughy interior. The *cajeta* is unlike any other caramel, boasting rich, earthy flavors. It takes time to make but is absolutely worth the effort.

THE AMERICAS · *Reaper*

TYPE: *CELEBRATORY*

 PREP TIME: 10 minutes for churros, 2 hours for cajeta
FRYING TIME: 20 minutes

 YIELD: 4 servings

 DIETARY: Vegetarian

CHURROS:

» ½ cup sugar, plus 1½ tablespoons more
» 1½ teaspoons ground cinnamon
» 2 tablespoons vegetable oil, plus more for frying
» 1 cup water
» ½ teaspoon salt
» 1 cup all-purpose flour

CAJETA:

» 1 quart goat milk
» 1 cup sugar
» 1 cinnamon stick
» ½ teaspoon salt
» 2 teaspoons vanilla extract
» ½ teaspoon baking soda

TO MAKE THE CHURROS:

1. Combine the ½ cup sugar with the ground cinnamon in a shallow bowl and set aside for coating the cooked churros.

2. Line a plate with paper towels and set near the stove. Pour the vegetable oil into a medium sauce pan so it is at least 2 inches deep. Begin heating the oil on medium heat to about 375°F.

3. Meanwhile, in a separate saucepan over medium heat, combine the water, remaining sugar, salt, 2 tablespoons of vegetable oil, and cook until the sugar has dissolved and the mixture is just about to boil. Remove from heat and stir in the flour, mixing until smooth. Transfer the warm dough into a piping bag fitted with a large star tip.

4. When the frying oil is hot, hold the piping bag over the pot and squeeze out a length of the churro mix to about 4 inches long, and then snip it off with scissors so it falls into the hot oil. Do this with several churros at a time, frying for just a couple of minutes until they're golden brown on all sides. Remove the cooked churros to the plate lined with paper towels to drain, and then roll them in the cinnamon sugar.

TO MAKE THE CAJETA:

5. Combine the goat milk and sugar in a tall saucepot over medium-high heat. Add the cinnamon stick, salt, and vanilla extract, and bring to a boil while stirring regularly, which should take around 10 minutes.

6. Remove from heat and add the baking soda, which will cause the mixture to rise and froth, but just keep stirring until it calms back down. Return to medium heat and cook for around 1 hour, stirring occasionally, until the whole mixture has thickened and turned a nice dark golden brown color.

7. Remove the cinnamon stick and continue to cook for another 20 to 40 minutes or so, stirring frequently to keep the bottom from burning. When the sauce is thick enough for your liking—we suggest it be thick enough to coat the back of a spoon—remove from heat and pour into a bowl for dipping. The caramel can also be covered and chilled to thicken it a little further.

"Revenge is sweet."

SCYTHE

As commander of Blackwatch, Gabriel Reyes had to make a number of complex and calculated decisions as his team embarked on its clandestine missions. When Reyes needed to wind down after a particularly difficult operation—such as the Venice Incident—he would mix up this concoction of Kahlúa, cinnamon whiskey, and triple sec.

TYPE: **DRINK**

PREP TIME: 5 minutes

YIELD: 1 serving

DIETARY: Gluten-Free, Vegetarian

» 1 ounce Kahlúa
» ½ ounce cinnamon whiskey
» ½ ounce triple sec
» Splash of grenadine
» A few drops angostura bitters

1. Add several ice cubes to a rocks glass, and then pour in the Kahlúa, cinnamon whiskey, and triple sec.

2. Add the splash of grenadine at the end for color, and finish with a few drops of bitters.

"Things are looking . . . grim."

MOLLETES

These open-faced bean-and-cheese sandwiches are both quick to make and easily adaptable to personal taste. The crispness of the bread supports the layer of refried beans and gooey cheese, while the salsa provides a welcome burst of acidity.

Although these snackable sandwiches can be a tad messy to eat, Sombra loves them; she often has a plate of them (or an empty plate) next to her keyboards and monitors in her hideout. The world's most talented hacker has to keep up her strength, after all, when there are conspiracies to unravel.

 COOKING TIME: 15 minutes   *YIELD:* 2 to 4 servings   *DIETARY:* None

» 3 medium sandwich rolls, such as bolillos, sliced lengthwise

» 3 tablespoons unsalted butter, softened

» One 16-ounce can refried beans

» 1 pound of chorizo, casings removed

» ½ cup shredded cheese such as mozzarella, Oaxaca, or cheddar

» ½ cup pico de gallo salsa, or other salsa of your choice

» 1 avocado, sliced

1. Spread the butter over the sliced rolls and toast under the broiler until just turning crisp and brown. Spread with refried beans and set aside.

2. In a medium frying pan, crumble the chorizo and cook over medium heat until browned, around 5 minutes. Pile the meat on top of the rolls and cover with cheese. Slip the rolls back under the broiler until the cheese has melted. Finally, top with some salsa and sliced avocado.

"We all have weaknesses . . ."

CONCHAS

These beautiful sweet buns are a lesser-known specialty of Panadería las Nieblas in Dorado. Their crunchy, colorful sugar crust resembles their seashell namesake. With soft dough and light flavors, they're perfect alongside a steaming cup of tea or coffee.

Sombra needs fuel for late-night hours hacking her enemies in her Dorado hideout. These buns are one of her go-to sweets to celebrate a successful mission, since she can pick them up from the neighborhood bakery. Nestled in front of her monitors, she can keep an eye on all of her latest schemes while nibbling on a dessert as sweet as victory.

 PREP TIME: 20 minutes
RISING TIME: 1 hour 30 minutes
BAKING TIME: 15 to 18 minutes

 YIELD: 12 conchas

 DIETARY: None

DOUGH:

» 1 cup warm whole milk

» ⅓ cup unsalted butter, melted (or ¼ cup lard)

» ⅓ cup sugar

» 2 teaspoons active dry yeast

» Pinch of salt

» 1 egg

» 3½ cups all-purpose flour, plus more for dusting

TOPPING:

» ¼ cup softened unsalted butter

» ⅓ cup granulated sugar

» ½ teaspoon vanilla extract

» ½ cup all-purpose flour

» Food coloring of your choice

TO MAKE THE DOUGH:

1. Stir together the warm milk, butter, and sugar in a large mixing bowl. Add the yeast, followed by the salt and egg. Gradually begin stirring in the flour a cup at a time until you have a dough that pulls away from the sides of the bowl and isn't overly sticky.

2. Turn out onto a lightly floured surface and knead for several minutes until the dough is soft and pliable; it should bounce back when poked. Place the dough back into its bowl, cover with plastic wrap, and set somewhere warm to rise for about 1 hour, or until doubled in size.

TO MAKE THE TOPPING:

3. While the dough rises, you can make your sugar paste. Mix together the butter, sugar, and vanilla until smooth. Add a little flour at a time until you have a thick paste that is still workable and doesn't fall apart. Divide the paste into three equal balls and mix in food coloring to your liking.

4. Roll out each ball of topping paste to a little under ¼ inch thick. Using a cookie cutter or a small glass, cut out 4 rounds about 1½ to 2 inches across of each color. Slide one disc at a time onto a spatula, then gently score it with decorative shapes using the cookie cutter, being careful not to cut all the way through if you can.

TO ASSEMBLE:

5. Preheat an oven to 375°F.

6. Once the dough has doubled in size, divide it into 12 equal pieces. Gently fold the pieces of dough over and pinch together on the bottom of each bun to form a smooth ball. Set these on a baking sheet lined with parchment paper, pinched side down, and brush their tops with water.

7. Slide a finished sugar paste round onto the top of a moistened bun. Repeat until all the buns are covered, and then let them rise for another 30 minutes or so.

8. Bake at 375°F for 15 to 18 minutes, until the buns are just turning golden. Let cool for a few minutes, and *BOOP!* You've got conchas!

PÃO DE QUEIJO

Light, fluffy, just shy of crunchy, and bursting with cheesy goodness, these little rolls are not to be missed. Unlike their French cousins, *gougères*, these cheese puffs are best eaten as they are, rather than filled. Because they are traditionally made with cassava flour rather than wheat flour, they are enjoying a renewed popularity among gluten-free eaters.

THE AMERICAS · *Lúcio*

TYPE: *PREP*

These puffs are quick to make and a staple in many Brazilian homes, Lúcio's included. He's even been known to snack on a few between recording sessions or take a batch to a hockey match.

» 1 cup whole milk

» ¼ cup vegetable oil

» ¼ cup unsalted butter

» 1 teaspoon salt

» 2 cups tapioca or cassava flour

» 2 eggs

» 1 cup grated Parmesan cheese

» ½ cup finely grated cheddar cheese

 PREP TIME: 10 minutes
BAKING TIME: 25 minutes

 YIELD: About 15 rolls

 DIETARY: Gluten-Free, Vegetarian

1. Preheat the oven to 425°F and line a baking sheet with parchment paper.

2. Combine the milk, oil, butter, and salt in a medium saucepan over medium heat. Bring to just under a boil, and then remove from heat and stir in the tapioca or cassava flour, making sure no dry lumps remain.

3. Transfer the dough to a medium-size mixing bowl. Beat the dough with a hand mixer for a minute or so to help it cool down slightly, and then beat in the eggs one at a time. When the eggs have been fully incorporated, beat in the cheese until the dough is evenly mixed with a smooth consistency.

4. Form the dough into spheres roughly the size of golf balls and space them out evenly on the prepared baking sheet.

5. Bake for about 25 minutes, or until the dough has puffed up and turned golden brown. Let cool for a minute or two before enjoying. Best eaten the same day, while still fresh.

"Come on, let's bring it together!"

MOQUECA

Moqueca is a delicious fish stew that is typically served with a *farofa*—a side dish made from toasted cassava flour—and sprinkled with a little bit of spicy *piri-piri* sauce. Growing up in the coastal city of Rio de Janeiro, Lúcio always had access to fresh fish, and this moqueca is one of his favorite ways to prepare the catch of the day.

PREP TIME: 15 minutes
MARINATING TIME: 25 minutes
COOKING TIME: 40 minutes

YIELD: 4 servings

DIETARY:
Gluten-Free

» 1 pound white fish fillet (cod, haddock, etc.), cubed

» Juice of 2 limes

» ¼ cup olive oil

» 1 medium yellow onion, diced

» 1 jalapeño pepper, seeded and sliced thin

» 3 cloves garlic, finely chopped

» 2 cups fish or chicken stock

» One 14-ounce can chopped tomatoes

» 1½ cups coconut milk

» Around 10 shrimp, deveined and tails removed

» Chopped coriander or parsley, to serve

1. Combine the fish cubes and lime juice in a small bowl. Let the fish marinate for 25 minutes.

2. Add the oil to a medium saucepan over medium heat. Add the onion, jalapeño, and garlic, and then cook for around 5 minutes, until fragrant and soft. Add the stock, chopped tomatoes, and coconut milk. Let this mixture come to a simmer and then cook, uncovered, for around 20 minutes. Finally, add the fish along with the lime juice and the shrimp to the pot.

3. Cook for another 10 minutes or so, until the fish and shrimp are cooked through. Serve hot and topped with chopped coriander or parsley.

"That's what I'm talking about."

BRIGADEIROS

These delightfully simple truffles originated as a method of drumming up support for a political candidate in post–World War II Brazil. At the time, fresh milk and sugar were scarce, so these chocolaty delights were made with condensed milk instead. Growing up, Lúcio considered these an extra-special treat because his father made them only on his birthday.

THE AMERICAS · Lúcio

TYPE: **CELEBRATORY**

BRIGADEIROS:

» 1 tablespoon unsalted butter, plus more for buttering bowl

» 3 tablespoons Dutch-process cocoa powder

» 14 ounces sweetened condensed milk

» Pinch of salt

TOPPINGS:

» Sprinkles

» Crushed nuts

» Shredded coconut

PREP TIME: 10 minutes
COOLING: 2 hours

YIELD: 12 brigadeiros

DIETARY: Gluten-Free, Vegetarian

1. Lightly butter a small mixing bowl and set aside. In a wide nonstick frying pan, combine the cocoa powder, condensed milk, butter, and salt. Place the pan over medium-low heat and begin gently stirring the mixture to melt the butter and combine the other ingredients. The mix is done when it has thickened considerably and begins to easily slide around the pan.

2. Remove from heat and transfer into the prepared mixing bowl. Let the mixture cool for at least an hour, although two hours would be better.

3. To form the brigadeiros, first set out a few small bowls of your desired toppings. Then, using a small spoon, scoop out some of the mixture and roll into a 1-inch ball. Roll in the desired toppings and place into a mini-cupcake paper. Repeat until the whole mixture has been used up. You can eat them right away, or chill until ready to enjoy.

"Let's up the tempo!"

LIMONADA

Sweet, creamy, and deeply refreshing, a cold glass of limonada is just what Lúcio needs to keep his energy up for a big open-air concert. In Brazil, limes are the citrus fruit of choice, but this sweet drink can also be made with lemons. After a particularly successful day, Lúcio will sometimes swap the condensed milk for cachaça and enjoy a caipirinha, Brazil's national cocktail. No matter how you decide to enjoy this beverage, good vibes are ensured.

THE AMERICAS · *Lúcio*

TYPE: **DRINK**

PREP TIME: 5 minutes

YIELD: 2 servings

DIETARY: Gluten-Free, Vegetarian

» **3 fresh limes**
» **⅓ cup sweetened condensed milk**
» **⅓ cup sugar**
» **3 to 4 cups cold water, to taste**

1. Zest the limes into a medium-size bowl or pitcher, then cut them in half and juice into the same container. Add the condensed milk, sugar, and 2 cups of the water, stirring to combine completely. Strain this into a pitcher, and then pour the remaining water (to taste) through the strainer. Stir together once more and serve in glasses with ice.

"Party on the objective, who's in?"

AFRICA

FATTOUSH SALAD

As one of the ranking members of Overwatch, Ana had little time to learn to cook between missions and training. This bright and refreshing salad is an efficient meal that Ana could put together and eat quickly before getting into her gear.

Fattoush salad features crisped pita bread as a topping—a great way to use leftover pita from another Egyptian or Mediterranean meal. Sumac, a spice common in the Middle East, is the star of this dish and should not be skipped; check your local Middle Eastern or Mediterranean market.

AFRICA • *Ana*

TYPE: *PREP*

SALAD:

» 1 round of pita, for crouton topping
» ¼ head iceberg lettuce, chopped
» 1 cup mint leaves, torn small
» 1 cup flat-leaf parsley, torn small
» 2 medium tomatoes, diced
» 1 cucumber, peeled and diced
» About ¼ cup feta cheese, or more to taste

DRESSING:

» 2 teaspoons sumac
» 1 to 2 tablespoons red wine vinegar
» ⅓ cup olive oil

 PREP TIME: 10 minutes

 YIELD: 1 to 2 servings

 DIETARY: Vegetarian

1. Preheat the oven to 350°F. Place the pita directly on the oven rack and bake until crisp, around 5 to 10 minutes. Break into pieces and set aside.

2. While the pita is baking, combine the greens for the salad in a large bowl, tossing together to make sure they are evenly mixed. Top with the tomatoes, cucumber, feta, and crispy pita when done.

3. Make up the dressing in a small bowl by combining the sumac, red wine vinegar, and olive oil. Drizzle the dressing over the salad to taste, and serve immediately.

"Someone needs to show how it's done."

LENTIL SOUP

Lentil soup is a reliable, hearty meal that will keep even the most unwavering military families feeling warm and peaceful all through the night. When Fareeha was younger, Ana would make this dish for the two of them after an intense day of martial arts training. Though she had little time to cook, Ana could put together a comforting lentil soup even on nights when Fareeha insisted she needed nothing. A mother always knows best.

AFRICA · *Ana*

TYPE: *COMFORT*

 PREP TIME: 5 minutes
COOKING TIME: 20 to 30 minutes

 YIELD: 4 servings

 DIETARY: Gluten-Free

- » 2 tablespoons unsalted butter
- » 1 large yellow onion, peeled and diced
- » 4 cloves garlic, peeled and diced
- » 1 medium carrot, diced
- » 1½ cups dried red lentils, rinsed
- » ¼ cup tomato paste
- » 1 teaspoon ground cumin
- » ½ teaspoon ground turmeric
- » 5 cups chicken stock
- » ½ cup heavy cream
- » Za'atar, Aleppo pepper, salt, pepper, or other seasonings such as thyme, oregano, or marjoram, to taste

1. In a medium saucepot, melt the butter over medium heat and add the onion and garlic. Cook for several minutes, until the onion is soft and fragrant and just beginning to turn golden.

2. Add the carrots, lentils, tomato paste, and spices, stirring to coat everything evenly. Add the chicken stock and bring to a simmer. Cook for about 20 to 30 minutes, or until the carrots are soft and the lentils have swelled and are bursting.

3. Turn the heat down to low and purée with an immersion blender. Stir in the cream, and then add the za'atar spice blend, Aleppo pepper, salt, pepper, or other seasonings to taste.

"Take your medicine."

UMM ALI

This Egyptian dessert is similar to a bread pudding but with a lighter texture and richly spiced. Flakes of puff pastry give it decadence, while morsels of nuts and raisins provide texture. This was Ana's favorite dessert as a child, and she later shared it with her daughter, Fareeha. Making it reminds Ana of happier days, before her nearly deadly encounter with Widowmaker.

AFRICA • *Ana*

TYPE: *CELEBRATORY*

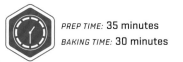

PREP TIME: 35 minutes
BAKING TIME: 30 minutes

YIELD: 4 to 6 servings

DIETARY: Vegetarian

» 1 package puff pastry, thawed
» 2 cups whole milk
» 2 cups heavy cream
» ½ cup sugar
» 1 teaspoon vanilla extract
» 1 teaspoon ground cinnamon
» ¼ teaspoon cardamom
» ¼ cup slivered almonds
» ¼ cup pistachios
» ¼ cup sultanas or raisins
» Butter, for baking pan

1. Preheat the oven to 425°F and set the puff pastry dough on a baking sheet lined with parchment paper. Bake the dough for about 10 to 15 minutes, or until the pastry is fully puffed up and golden brown.

2. While the pastry is baking, warm up the milk, cream, and sugar in a small saucepan over medium heat. Stir gently until the sugar has dissolved, and then add the vanilla and spices. Remove from heat.

3. Remove the puff pastry from the oven and set aside to cool, but leave the oven on. Once cooled, break the pastry into bite-size pieces and set aside.

4. Lightly butter a 9-by-12-inch pan and add a generous layer of crumbled pastry to the bottom. Add a layer of the nuts and sultanas or raisins, then more pastry, and repeat, until the dish is heaping. Gently pour in the milk mixture, taking care not to overfill. Let this mixture sit for about 10 minutes, then add more milk if needed.

5. Bake this dish for about 15 minutes, until fragrant and golden brown.

"Mother knows best."

BAKED KIBBEH

With a slightly crunchy crust, savory spiced filling, and moist consistency, this lamb pie is delicious with rice or mashed potatoes. With Ana gone, Pharah is left to make this recipe herself when she is looking for comfort. Occasionally she will share it with her friends and family to keep her mother's memory alive.

AFRICA • *Pharah*

TYPE: *COMFORT*

- › 2 pounds ground lamb
- › ½ teaspoon ground cinnamon
- › ½ teaspoon cardamom
- › ½ teaspoon allspice
- › ½ teaspoon cumin
- › 1 teaspoon salt
- › Splash of olive oil
- › 1 medium yellow onion, minced
- › ½ pound cracked bulgur wheat, soaked overnight
- › 1 egg

 SOAKING TIME: 8 hours or overnight
PREP TIME: 35 minutes
BAKING TIME: 1 hour

 YIELD: 6 to 8 servings

 DIETARY: None

1. Preheat the oven to 350°F and set aside a pie dish. Mix the lamb with the cinnamon, cardamom, allspice, cumin, and salt in a large mixing bowl, and then divide the meat in half.

2. In a medium frying pan, heat a splash of olive oil over medium heat and brown the onion. Add only half of the spiced meat to the pan and brown that as well. Transfer the cooked meat and onion to a bowl to cool.

3. In a separate bowl, take the uncooked meat and mix with the bulgur wheat and the egg. Divide this meat mixture in half, spread half of it along the bottom of the pie dish, and then heap the cooked meat on top of it.

4. Finally, take the last of the uncooked meat and gently spread it over the middle layer. Using a sharp knife, cut the kibbeh in a decorative pattern. Pour the olive oil over the top and bake for 1 hour.

"Culinary superiority achieved."

CANADIAN BUTTER TARTS

With a shortbread crust and a light, nutty topping, Canadian butter tarts make an excellent accompaniment to a nice steaming mug of tea. In this recipe, we use a baking tray instead of individually prepared tart shells, which makes this recipe easier to prep for small gatherings.

These tarts were Pharah's favorite part of the time she spent in Canada during her childhood. While her relationship with her father, Sam, was complicated then, she has come to enjoy sharing this special treat with him during the holidays. Their warm spiciness fends off the winter chill, no matter where she finds herself.

AFRICA · *Pharah*

TYPE: *CELEBRATORY*

PREP TIME: 5 minutes
BAKING TIME: 25 minutes

YIELD: About 16 squares

DIETARY: Vegetarian

CRUST:

- ½ cup unsalted butter
- 1 cup all-purpose flour
- 2 tablespoons packed dark brown sugar
- ¼ cup rolled oats

FILLING:

- ½ cup walnuts
- ½ cup unsalted butter, softened
- 2 eggs
- 1 cup packed dark brown sugar
- 2 tablespoons maple syrup
- ½ teaspoon vanilla extract
- ¼ teaspoon salt
- ½ teaspoon baking powder
- Powdered sugar for dusting

TO MAKE THE CRUST:

1. Butter and lightly flour an 8-inch square baking pan and preheat the oven to 350°F. Rub the butter into the flour, brown sugar, and oats for the crust until you have a nice, soft, and crumbly mixture. Press this into the bottom of the prepared pan, and then bake for 5 minutes. Remove the pan from the oven and set nearby.

TO MAKE THE FILLING:

2. Pulse the walnuts in a food processor to a fine consistency. In a medium mixing bowl, stir together the walnuts, butter, eggs, brown sugar, maple syrup, vanilla, salt, and baking powder, and then pour over the crust. Bake for an additional 20 minutes.

3. Allow to cool slightly before cutting into squares with a buttered knife. Dust with powdered sugar if you like, and enjoy with tea or coffee.

"Butter tart? That sounds dangerous."

SAHLAB

Smooth and creamy, with rich spices and a nutty topping, this relaxing beverage is traditionally enjoyed in the winter and warms you up from the core.

Pharah went against her mother's wishes and forged her own path to become the brave and dedicated soldier she is today. Pharah makes sahlab the way her mother, Ana, taught her and occasionally dreams of sitting down with her mother to share a cup.

AFRICA • *Pharah*

TYPE: *DRINK*

 **COOKING TIME:** 5 minutes

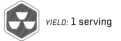 **YIELD:** 1 serving

 **DIETARY:** Gluten-Free, Vegetarian

» 2 cups whole milk

» 2 tablespoons arrowroot or cornstarch

» 3 teaspoons sugar

» Dash of vanilla extract

» ½ teaspoon ground cinnamon, plus more for topping

» ¼ teaspoon ground ginger

» Finely chopped pistachios (optional)

1. Combine milk, arrowroot, sugar, vanilla extract, cinnamon, and ginger in a small saucepan over medium heat. While whisking, allow the milk to come to a simmer. Cook for around 3 to 5 minutes, until the whole mixture has thickened.

2. Remove from heat and strain into serving mug. Top with extra cinnamon, and pistachios, if using.

TIP: The drink is generally enjoyed hot in winter but can also be iced in hot weather.

"Remember your training, and we'll get through this just fine."

JOLLOF RICE

Satisfying but not heavy, both festive and familiar, this Nigerian staple is comfort food at its very best. It is the wholesome heart of every family gathering, with a spicy kick to warm everyone up. A Scotch bonnet pepper is not for the faint of heart, so those who would like a less spicy version should omit it.

This dish was part of Doomfist's routine before martial arts competitions in his youth, and his family's chefs knew to always have a plate ready for him. Now that he has changed "occupations," it fills a similar role in preparing him for completing new objectives.

 PREP TIME: 15 minutes
COOKING TIME: 50 minutes

 YIELD: 6 to 8 large servings

 *DIETARY:* Gluten-Free

» One 16-ounce can diced tomatoes (preferably fire roasted)

» 4 cloves garlic

» 1 medium red onion, roughly chopped

» 1 medium red bell pepper, stemmed, cored, and roughly chopped

» 1 Scotch bonnet pepper (optional)

» 2 tablespoons unsalted butter

» ¼ cup peanut oil

» 1 teaspoon curry powder

» ½ teaspoon thyme

» ½ teaspoon ground ginger

» 1 teaspoon paprika

» 2 to 3 raw chicken breasts, diced

» ½ cup tomato paste

» 2 cups uncooked white rice

» 2 ½ cups chicken stock

1. Combine the diced tomatoes, garlic, onion, bell pepper, and Scotch bonnet (if using) in a food processor. Pulse several times until the texture is fine, and then set aside the resulting tomato mixture.

2. In a medium frying pan over medium heat, melt the butter with the peanut oil. When the butter is melted, add the spices, then the cubed chicken. Stir for several minutes, until the chicken is browned on all sides.

3. Add the chicken, tomato mixture, tomato paste, white rice, and chicken stock to a large saucepan. Bring to a boil, stirring occasionally to make sure the rice doesn't stick to the bottom of the pan. Reduce heat to low, cover, and cook for about 20 minutes, until the rice is soft. Take the pot off the heat and let sit, covered, for another 10 minutes. Fluff the rice with a fork and serve hot.

"I am just getting started!"

SHUKU SHUKU

Though Doomfist is wholly focused on changing the world through the influence of Talon, even he has fond memories of these sweets from his childhood. These morsels are crunchy on the outside and chewy within, with a slight sweetness and a lingering aftertaste of coconut. Quick and easy to make, they're a great dessert to share anywhere, including at clandestine meetings for plotting the next world conflict.

AFRICA • *Doomfist*

TYPE: *CELEBRATORY*

PREP TIME: 5 minutes
BAKING TIME: 20 minutes

YIELD: 12 servings

DIETARY: Vegetarian

» 1 cup unsweetened flaked coconut

» ¼ cup fine sugar

» 3 egg yolks

» ½ teaspoon baking powder

» ½ cup all-purpose flour

1. Preheat the oven to 350°F and line a baking sheet with parchment paper.

2. In a small mixing bowl, combine the coconut, sugar, egg yolks, and baking powder until a nice even mixture forms. Shape into 1-inch balls, and then roll each one in the flour before setting on the baking sheet. Leave a few inches between each round as they expand while baking.

3. Bake for 20 minutes, or until just starting to turn golden brown on the edges.

"You don't want to get in the way of this."

PUNCH DRUNK PUNCH

This refreshing punch bursts with a citrus zing that perfectly complements a hot summer day. Based on a traditional Chapman, it is wildly flavorful and quick to make.

As far as Doomfist is concerned, there's no better way to fix your problems than with a good strong punch. While many swear by the addition of rum, he prefers gin, which he considers more sophisticated.

AFRICA • *Doomfist*

TYPE: *DRINK*

PREP TIME: 5 minutes

YIELD: 1 serving

DIETARY: Gluten-Free, Vegetarian

» Ice
» A few slices each lemon, lime, and cucumber
» 1 cup orange soda
» 1 cup lemon-lime soda
» A few drops angostura bitters
» Splash of grenadine (or cassis)

1. Fill a highball glass halfway with ice and the slices of citrus and cucumber. Add the two sodas and the bitters.

2. Finally, add the grenadine over the top. (Swap the grenadine for cassis for some added complexity.)

TIP: To make an alcoholic version, add 2 ounces of gin or rum.

"One punch is all I need."

73

PUFF PUFFS

A popular snack in West African countries, this deep-fried treat can be served for breakfast or as a side dish. The slight crunch of the outside and soft fluff of the inside make a delightful duo that rivals even the partnership of Efi and Orisa. The youthful engineer and her faithful omnic companion have been known to enjoy these delicious morsels before heading into their innovation-filled mornings.

AFRICA • *Orisa*

TYPE: *PREP*

» 2 cups warm water

» 2 teaspoons instant dry yeast

» 3 ½ cups all-purpose flour

» ½ cup sugar

» 1 teaspoon salt

» Vegetable oil for deep frying

» Powdered sugar for dusting

PREP TIME: 5 minutes
RISING TIME: 1 hour
FRYING TIME: 15 minutes

YIELD: Around 24 puff puffs

DIETARY: Vegan

1. Combine the water, yeast, flour, sugar, and salt in a large mixing bowl until you have a thick mixture that is somewhat soupy. Cover loosely with plastic and set somewhere warm to rise for around 1 hour, or until it has doubled in size.

2. When you are ready to make the puff puffs, bring a deep pot filled with at least 2 inches of vegetable oil up to around 350°F over medium-high heat.

3. Using an oiled hand or a small ice-cream scoop, squeeze or drop balls of dough into the hot oil, about 1 tablespoon at a time. Let the dough balls cook for around 1 minute on each side, flipping them once, until they are a nice dark golden brown. Use a skimmer or slotted spoon to remove the cooked puff puffs, and let them drain on a plate lined with paper towels.

4. To serve, sprinkle with a little powdered sugar.

"I'm still new at this."

ORISA SUNDAE

It used to be that nobody had ever heard of Efi Oladele. Now, thanks to the Adawe Foundation's grant for her work in robotics, she enjoys a bit more prominence. Efi was first served this amazing sundae in celebration of her most notable robotic achievement so far: the reconfigured OR15 defense robot, named Orisa. Orisa is almost as famous as Efi, though she is still learning her place among the citizens of Numbani.

 PREP TIME: 5 minutes

 YIELD: 1 serving

 DIETARY: Vegetarian

» 1 pint chocolate
  ice cream

» 1 banana, peeled and
  cut in half

» 1 kiwi fruit, peeled and sliced

» 1 round wafer cookie

» 1 dark chocolate square for
  eyes, cut into slices

» Caramel sauce (see tip below)

» 1 maraschino cherry

1. Begin by filling your serving dish with two to three scoops of chocolate ice cream, depending on the size of dish. Then gently place the two pieces of banana on opposite sides of the ice cream in the dish, and add a big scoop of ice cream over the top to hold them down.

2. Set a couple of kiwi slices around the back of the "head," along with the wafer cookie. Insert two pieces of chocolate for Orisa's eyes, and then drizzle with caramel sauce and top with a cherry!

TIP: You can use a commercially available caramel sauce, or the sauce from Tracer's Sticky Toffee Pudding recipe (see page 83) or the cajeta from Reaper's Churros with Cajeta (see page 35).

"This is much better than winning the science fair!"

HIBISCUS TEA

This herbal tea is as sweet as its deep pink color suggests and can be served hot or iced. It's a popular drink in Numbani for both kids and adults, and it's Efi's drink of choice while she's tinkering in her workshop. In the summer, Efi will sip on an iced glass of hibiscus tea while she and Orisa listen to Lúcio's music and the hum of the City of Harmony.

AFRICA · *Orisa*

TYPE: *DRINK*

 PREP TIME: 10 minutes

 YIELD: 2 servings

 DIETARY: Gluten-Free, Vegan

» ½ cup dried hibiscus flowers

» 3 cups water

» ¼ cup sugar, or to taste

» Fresh mint (optional)

» 1 teaspoon freshly grated ginger (optional)

» Orange peel (optional)

» Dash of vanilla extract

1. Combine the hibiscus, water, and sugar in a small saucepan. Bring to a simmer while stirring, and then remove from heat. Add additional flavorings, if using, for a more complex flavor, and allow to steep for about 10 minutes.

2. Strain into a clean container and add the vanilla. Serve warm, or chilled over ice.

"Your safety is my primary concern."

EUROPE

STICKY TOFFEE PUDDING

No matter how shiny your outlook, it's impossible to keep a stiff upper lip every single day. On days when she's feeling a little blue, Tracer will put together this homey pudding and curl up by the window. Sticky toffee pudding is a holiday staple in England, and it never fails to remind her what she is fighting for every day.

EUROPE · *Tracer*

TYPE: *PREP*

 **PREP TIME:** 15 minutes
BAKING TIME: 35 minutes

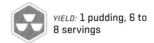 *YIELD:* 1 pudding, 6 to 8 servings

 DIETARY: Vegetarian

PUDDING:

- ½ cup unsalted butter, softened
- ½ cup packed light brown sugar
- 2 eggs
- 1 teaspoon baking powder
- 1 teaspoon baking soda
- 1 tablespoon ground ginger
- 3 tablespoons black treacle or molasses
- 1 cup all-purpose flour
- 1 cup whole milk
- Vanilla ice cream, to serve (optional)

SAUCE:

- 3½ ounces unsalted butter
- 1 cup packed light brown sugar
- 1 tablespoon black treacle or molasses
- 1 cup heavy cream
- 1 teaspoon vanilla extract

TO MAKE THE PUDDING:

1. Preheat the oven to 350°F and lightly butter an 8-by-8-inch cake pan.

2. In a large mixing bowl or stand mixer, beat together the butter and brown sugar until smooth, and then beat in the eggs, baking powder, baking soda, ginger, and treacle. When those are combined, beat in the flour. Finally, add the milk and beat until just mixed.

3. Pour into the prepared baking pan and bake for 35 minutes, until the middle still has a little wobble but the edges are set.

TO MAKE THE SAUCE:

4. While the pudding is baking, make the sauce. Combine all the sauce ingredients in a small saucepan and stir occasionally over medium-low heat until the sugar has dissolved. Bring to a bubble, cook for a few more minutes, and then remove from heat.

5. To serve, turn out the hot pudding onto a serving dish. Cut into slices, and then top with vanilla ice cream, if using, and a generous drizzle of the sauce over it all. Enjoy warm.

"Right on target."

BEER-BATTERED FISH AND CHIPS

Light and crispy beer-battered cod with delicious thick-cut chips has become an iconic and quintessentially British dish. Tracer has traveled all over the world and across time, but fish and chips has always been her favorite dish no matter where she's been. She got this particular recipe from the chippy just outside King's Row called Bell Fish and Chips.

EUROPE • *Tracer*

TYPE: *COMFORT*

- 2 cups all-purpose flour
- 1 tablespoon baking powder
- 1 teaspoon salt, plus more for serving
- ¼ teaspoon cayenne pepper
- One 12-ounce bottle brown ale or amber beer
- 1½ pounds firm-fleshed whitefish (cod works great), cut into 1-inch strips
- Cornstarch, for dredging
- 2 to 4 cups vegetable oil

PREP TIME: 20 minutes
FRYING TIME: 20 minutes

YIELD: 4 servings

DIETARY: None

1. In a medium-size mixing bowl, combine the dry ingredients, and then whisk in the beer until the batter is smooth. Let sit for about 20 minutes. Fill a small bowl with cornstarch and set aside.

2. Heat the oil to around 350°F in a frying pan with tall sides. Line a plate with paper towels and set aside.

3. Dip the strips of fish into the cornstarch, then into the batter. Working with only a couple of pieces at a time, lower the battered fish into the hot oil. Cook on both sides, about 2 minutes total, until crispy and golden brown. Remove the strips and lay them on the paper towel-lined plate to drain. Repeat until all the strips are fried.

4. Serve with fries, malt vinegar, and a good amount of salt.

"The world could always use more chippies!"

BATTENBERG CAKE

Based on a traditional Victorian-era tea cake, this is an ideal afternoon snack for the upstanding citizen. This particular version, popular with tourists as well as locals, is served during high tea at the Alderworth Hotel.

With all the effort it takes to go zipping through time, Tracer likes to indulge in sweet treats once in a while to keep her energy up. She likes to share this extra-special treat with her girlfriend, Emily, after a matinee at the cinema.

EUROPE • *Tracer*

TYPE: *CELEBRATORY*

 PREP TIME: 15 minutes
BAKING TIME: 25 minutes
ASSEMBLY AND CHILLING TIME: 1 hour 30 minutes

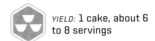 YIELD: 1 cake, about 6 to 8 servings

 DIETARY: Vegetarian

» 1 cup unsalted butter, softened, plus an extra couple of tablespoons for greasing the pan

» ¾ cup sugar

» 3 eggs

» 1 teaspoon vanilla extract

» 1 teaspoon baking powder

» ½ teaspoon salt

» ¼ cup whole milk

» 1½ cups all-purpose flour

» Orange and blue food coloring

» ⅓ cup apricot jam, warmed

» 7 ounces marzipan

1. Preheat the oven to 400°F and prepare a loaf pan by greasing the pan with a couple of tablespoons of butter and then folding a piece of aluminum foil in half and placing it widthwise in the middle of the pan to divide it into two equal halves.

2. In a large mixing bowl, cream together the butter and sugar until fluffy and smooth. Add the eggs, one at a time, until they are also incorporated. Add the vanilla, baking powder, and salt, followed by the milk. Gradually add the flour, mixing just until everything has come together in a thick batter.

3. Divide the batter equally between two bowls and add your desired colors (Tracer's suggestions are orange and blue). Pour these mixtures into each half of the divided loaf pan and bake for 25 minutes, or until the cakes are set and a toothpick inserted into the middle of each comes out clean. Let cool completely.

4. Once the cakes have cooled, remove them from the pan. Using a sharp serrated knife, cut both cakes so they are the same size, trimming off the sides and tops to make flat sides and equal-size cakes. Next, cut each of the trimmed cakes in half lengthwise.

5. Beginning with one of the cake logs, brush it all over with the warmed apricot jam, and then repeat the process and place a second log, of the other color, next to the first. Repeat with the remaining two logs, and stack on top of the first two. This should result in a checkerboard effect.

6. Finally, roll out the marzipan as thin as you can without compromising its strength. Brush one side of the marzipan with the remaining jam, and then carefully drape it over the prepared cake, jam side down. Trim off any excess and tuck the seams under one of the long sides; this will be the bottom of the cake. Chill for about an hour to help the whole cake set, and then cut into slices to serve.

"Keep calm and Tracer on."

FULL IRISH BREAKFAST

Whether you're a scientist, medic, or mechanic, everyone needs a good breakfast to start the day right. Moira is often consumed by her work, but when it comes to a full breakfast spread, she can put it away as well as anyone. Topped off with a couple of fried eggs, this breakfast consists of pudding slices, a type of Irish sausage, fried crisp, with savory beans and mushrooms. Wash it down with a strong cup of coffee for a robust start to the day.

The number of components makes this a slightly tricky meal to make, but with a little coordination and practice, you'll have it on the table in no time.

 PREP TIME: 30 minutes

 YIELD: 1 large serving

DIETARY: None

- » 2 banger sausages
- » ½ of a 16-ounce can of baked beans
- » 1 tablespoon oil
- » 2 slices back bacon
- » 6 to 8 ¼-inch slices black pudding
- » 6 to 8 ¼-inch slices white pudding
- » 2 eggs
- » 1 tomato, sliced in halves or wedges
- » 2 slices soda bread, toasted and buttered
- » Optional additions: potato hash, fried mushrooms, bubble and squeak, potato farl, and boxty

1. Fill a small frying pan with about 1 inch of water and set over medium-high heat. Add the bangers to the pan, cover, and let cook until the rest of the meal is finished, about 20 to 30 minutes.

2. Meanwhile, in a separate small saucepan, heat the baked beans over low heat until they are hot. Keep warm until ready to plate.

3. In a large frying pan over medium heat, spread the tablespoon of oil across the bottom. Crowd in the bacon and pudding slices, and cook for 5 to 10 minutes, flipping at least once, until the pudding is crispy and the bacon is cooked through. Transfer to a plate and keep warm.

4. Into half of the same pan, crack the two eggs and cook however you like them (Moira likes hers sunny-side up). On the other side of the pan, fry the tomato slices for about a minute, until slightly softened.

5. When everything is done, plate it all together and serve straight away.

"Better living through science."

GUINNESS STEW

Nothing drives out a chill or malaise like comfort food from your childhood. This rich, flavorful gravy bursts with vegetables and tender bites of meat. It's wonderful on its own or served over mashed potatoes for a little extra body.

Though Moira typically prefers the science of baking over the art of cooking, she used to enjoy this dish during many a Sunday family dinner, and she still seeks solace in its warmth and comforting fullness. Even in the faraway laboratories of Oasis, she can still put together this little piece of Dublin for herself.

PREP TIME: 30 minutes
STEWING TIME: 2 hours

YIELD: 4 servings

DIETARY: None

» 4 slices bacon, cut into small pieces

» 1 pound stew beef, cut into bite-size pieces

» 1 leek, white and pale green parts sliced thin

» 2 cloves garlic, minced

» 1 tablespoon all-purpose flour

» 12 ounces dark stout beer

» 1 tablespoon tomato paste

» 4 sprigs fresh thyme

» 2 to 3 medium carrots, cut into 1-inch pieces

» 1 large potato, peeled and chopped into 1-inch pieces

» 1 teaspoon packed dark brown sugar

» 3 cups chicken stock

» Salt and pepper, to taste

1. Cook the bacon over medium heat in a medium frying pan until it is brown and crisp. Remove the bacon and add it to a waiting soup pot, keeping about 1 tablespoon bacon fat in the frying pan.

2. Add the stew beef to the frying pan and brown the meat on all sides. When done, transfer the meat to the soup pot. Next, add the leek and garlic to the frying pan and cook until soft and starting to brown, about 5 minutes. Toss the flour into the pan and stir to incorporate. Transfer the leek-and-garlic mixture to the soup pot, and then add all the remaining ingredients to the soup pot.

3. Bring the soup pot up to a boil, and then cover and reduce the heat to low. Simmer for 2 hours, or until the meat is tender. Once the stew has simmered for a while, add salt and pepper to taste. Serve alongside bread and butter, mashed potatoes, or both.

"I will allow none to stand in the way of progress."

BARMBRACK

Barmbrack is a bread speckled with dried fruits that is popular in Ireland around Halloween. Slices are particularly delicious toasted, with a daub of good butter. Moira has been known to make a loaf after a day in the lab, and she occasionally alters this original recipe to a version that hews more to the tastes of Oasis by doubling the candied ginger and swapping the currants for diced dates.

EUROPE · *Moira*

TYPE: *CELEBRATORY*

PREP TIME: 15 minutes
RISING TIME: 1 hour 30 minutes
BAKING TIME: 30 minutes
COOLING TIME: 15 minutes

YIELD: 1 loaf

DIETARY: Vegetarian

- » 2 teaspoons dried yeast
- » ¾ cup warm whole milk
- » 2 tablespoons sugar
- » 2½ cups all-purpose flour, divided
- » Pinch of salt
- » ½ teaspoon ground cinnamon
- » ¼ teaspoon nutmeg
- » ¼ cup unsalted butter, melted
- » 1 cup golden raisins
- » ½ cup dried currants
- » ¼ cup mixed candied lemon or orange peel, diced
- » ¼ cup diced candied ginger
- » 1 egg
- » ¼ cup heavy cream, for glazing

1. Combine the yeast, warm milk, sugar, and ½ cup of the flour in a medium-size mixing bowl. Add the salt, cinnamon, and nutmeg, followed by the melted butter, dried fruit, candied fruit, candied ginger, and the egg. Gradually mix in the remaining 2 cups flour, switching from using a spoon to your hands as needed as the dough comes together.

2. When most of the flour has been incorporated, turn out the dough onto a clean work surface. Knead for several minutes until you have a pliable dough that bounces back when poked. Place this dough into a lightly buttered clean bowl and cover loosely with plastic wrap or a damp towel. Leave in a warm place for about 1 hour to double in size.

3. Once the dough has risen, punch it back down and form into a loaf shape. At this point, you can place the bread in a lightly buttered loaf pan or on a baking sheet. Cover and let rise again for 30 minutes. After the dough has risen for the second time, brush it with a little heavy cream, and then bake for 30 minutes, or until the top has turned dark golden. Let cool for at least 15 minutes before slicing.

"Humanity is bedeviled by the mysteries of creation."

IRISH COFFEE

It makes sense that Irish coffee began as an impromptu drink for travelers: It offers a little pick-me-up, a little relaxation, and a little inspiration. Turns out it's also perfect for jump-starting the brain while pulling an all-nighter on groundbreaking genetics research. Moira developed a taste for the spiced coffee served in Oasis, but it was missing the *uisce beatha*, the "water of life" from her home in Dublin. She adapted the recipe to her own preferences, fiddling with the proportions until they were just to her liking—and the result might just be the key to her next big discovery.

EUROPE • *Moira*

TYPE: *DRINK*

PREP TIME: 5 minutes

YIELD: 1 serving

DIETARY: Gluten-Free, Vegetarian

- » 1 teaspoon packed dark brown sugar
- » 1 ounce Irish whiskey
- » 2 cups freshly brewed coffee
- » ½ cup whipping cream
- » ½ teaspoon ground cardamom
- » ¼ teaspoon ground ginger

1. Put the brown sugar in the bottom of a heatproof glass or mug, and then pour the whiskey over. Swirl to dissolve the sugar, and then pour in the coffee.

2. In a small bowl, quickly whip together the cream and spices with a whisk until the cream is fluffy but not quite stiff. Gently spoon some of this onto the top of the coffee. Enjoy as is, or stir the cream into the hot coffee. Drink immediately.

"Sláinte."

KROPPKAKOR

These soft, pillowy dumplings with richly flavored filling are a traditional dish in Sweden. As one of the most brilliant engineers in the world, Torbjörn has a particular liking for this because the recipe can easily be tinkered with. The only requisite step is that the dumplings be boiled. Everything else—from the fillings and toppings to the type of flour and the potato-preparation method—is up for debate, but he's fairly fond of the recipe below.

EUROPE • *Torbjörn*

TYPE: *COMFORT*

PREP TIME: 20 minutes
COOKING TIME: 20 to 40 minutes

YIELD: Around 18 dumplings

DIETARY: None

» 5 medium-size potatoes, peeled and chopped

» 1 egg

» 1 teaspoon salt, plus more for boiling

» ½ medium yellow onion, diced

» ½ pound bacon or salt pork

» 2 teaspoon ground allspice

» 2 to 3 cups all-purpose flour

» 2 tablespoons unsalted butter for frying (optional)

» Lingonberry jam for serving (optional)

1. Bring a large pot of water to a boil, and then add the potatoes. Cook the potatoes until fork tender, and then drain completely and transfer to a bowl.

2. Mash the potatoes, and then add the egg and salt to the hot mash while stirring rapidly. When this mixture is fully mixed, let it sit until it is cool enough to handle.

3. While the potatoes are cooling, make the filling. Combine the onion and bacon in a frying pan and cook for several minutes, until the onions are soft and golden brown and the bacon is just shy of crispy. Remove to a separate bowl, reserving the grease, and mix in the allspice.

4. Set another large pot of salted water on the stove to boil. Once the potato mix is cool enough to touch, mix in the flour a half cup at a time until you have a thick dough consistency that isn't sticky.

5. Knead a few times in the bowl, and then begin pinching off pieces a little bigger than a golf ball. Flatten each ball into a disk, and then spoon about 2 teaspoons of the bacon-and-onion mix onto the middle of it. Fold the edges of the dough around the meat to cover it completely, and then roll into a slightly flattened ball to seal the edges. The filling should be completely enclosed with none oozing out. Set aside and repeat until you have used up all the filling and potato.

6. Working in batches, drop several dumplings into the boiling water. Let them cook for several minutes, until they float back up to the top. Remove to a plate to cool. You can either enjoy the dumplings straightaway after boiling, or you can fry them in the bacon grease and butter for several minutes, until golden brown on each side. Serve hot with a side of lingonberry jam.

"A marvel of culinary engineering!"

INGRID'S APPLE PIE

Torbjörn isn't the only genius in the house. His wife, Ingrid, is a brilliant chemical engineer who has passed her inquisitive nature on to her daughter. Ingrid has engineered some kitchen marvels as well, including this Swedish take on apple pie. Not only does it fill the house with enticing scents as it bakes, but its textures and flavors are perfectly constructed: A sweet almond crumble balances tart apples, while slivered almonds provide textural complexity against the soft crust and filling. This flavorful pie has won acclaim near and far and is a favorite of family friend Mercy.

EUROPE • *Torbjörn*

TYPE: *CELEBRATORY*

PREP TIME: 25 minutes
CHILLING TIME: 1 hour
BAKING TIME: 40 minutes
COOLING TIME: 15 minutes

YIELD: 1 pie, about 8 servings

DIETARY: Vegetarian

CRUST:

» 1½ cups all-purpose flour

» 1 to 2 tablespoons sugar

» ½ cup (1 stick) unsalted butter, chilled

» Cold water, roughly ¼ cup

FILLING:

» 4 tart apples, cored and peeled

» 1 teaspoon ground cinnamon

» ½ teaspoon ground allspice

» ½ teaspoon cardamom

» ¼ cup packed light brown sugar

» ¼ cup all-purpose flour

» ½ cup sliced almonds

TOPPING:

» 2 tablespoons unsalted butter, chilled

» 3 ounces marzipan

» ½ cup all-purpose flour

» ½ cup packed light brown sugar

» Heavy cream, for brushing

TO MAKE THE CRUST:

1. In a medium-size mixing bowl, rub together the flour, sugar, and butter until you have a coarse mixture with no large lumps. Gradually add just enough cold water to bring the dough together, but don't overwork it. Wrap in plastic and chill for at least 1 hour.

2. When chilled, roll out the dough fairly thin, to about ⅛ to ¼ inch thick, and drape over a pie pan. Trim off any excess dough and save for the lattice.

TO MAKE THE FILLING AND ASSEMBLE:

3. Slice the apples thin, no more than ¼ inch thick. In a medium-size mixing bowl, toss slices with the cinnamon, allspice, cardamom, brown sugar, flour, and almonds until completely coated. Spread the filling evenly over the pie crust, shaking the dish a little to help the slices settle.

4. Preheat the oven to 375°F.

5. In a food processor, pulse together the two tablespoons of butter along with the marzipan, flour, and brown sugar until you have a nice even consistency; if any large pieces remain, crumble them up by hand. Sprinkle this mixture over the apple filling, and then cut long strips from the remaining pie crust dough. Lay these over the pie in a lattice pattern, and then brush the crust with a little heavy cream.

6. Bake for around 40 minutes, until the crust has turned golden and the filling has settled somewhat. Let cool for at least 15 minutes before slicing. Enjoy with a little heavy cream drizzled over a slice or vanilla ice cream on the side.

"Den är paj."

GLÖGG

Nearly every Swedish family has their own secret recipe for glögg, and the Lindholms are no exception. While some recipes call for rum or port, this is a simpler version, relying on brandy for the extra kick. It's a delicious and warming drink, very popular around the winter holidays.

TYPE: *DRINK*

PREP TIME: 10 minutes
STEEPING TIME: 1 hour

YIELD: About 4 to 6 servings

DIETARY: Gluten-Free, Vegan

» One 750-milliliter bottle red wine (blends work well)
» ½ cup sugar, or more to taste
» Peel of an orange
» 2 tablespoons dark raisins
» 2 tablespoons blanched almonds
» 2 teaspoons ground cardamom
» 2-to-3-inch piece fresh ginger, sliced thin
» 2 cinnamon sticks
» ¼ teaspoon ground cloves
» 1 cup brandy
» Orange slice to garnish (optional)

1. Combine all the ingredients, except the orange slice, in a medium saucepan over medium heat. Bring to a simmer and cook for a couple of minutes, and then remove from heat, cover, and let sit for around an hour to allow the flavors to meld.

2. Strain slowly into a clean pot, letting the dregs that have settled to the bottom of the pot stay there. Discard the cinnamon stick, ginger, and orange peel, but reserve the raisins and almonds to use as a garnish.

3. Serve the glögg hot in heatproof mugs or sturdy cups, garnished with a slice of orange and about 2 teaspoons of the raisins and almonds per serving.

"Do you appreciate my craftsmanship?"

TOAST SKAGEN

This easy recipe is a common appetizer in Sweden, which has a rich history of fishing. Dill, the classic Scandinavian herb, brings a bold flavor to the creamy sauce, making these surprisingly delectable offerings for a party. Not one for fancy soirees, Brigitte prefers to enjoy her toasts as a snack between repairing armor and mulling over new designs with her father. Even now, when facing a particularly challenging technical problem, Brigitte often relies on a batch of toast Skagen to help her work through it.

EUROPE · *Brigitte*

TYPE: *PREP*

» 4 slices white bread

» 2 tablespoons unsalted butter, softened

» 11 ounces extra small or small shrimp, cooked

» 4 tablespoons mayonnaise

» 1 tablespoon Dijon mustard

» 2 tablespoons freshly chopped dill, plus more for garnish

» 5 ounces pink or orange caviar, for garnish

» Lemon wedges

 PREP TIME: 10 minutes

 YIELD: 16 slices

 DIETARY: None

1. Trim the crusts off the slices of bread, and then spread both sides with a thin layer of butter. Fry the bread on both sides in a frying pan over medium heat until golden and crisped. Cut into triangles and set aside.

2. Mix together the shrimp, mayonnaise, mustard, and dill in a small bowl, and then divide the topping among the toast slices. Top with a little caviar and garnish with extra dill. Give the toasts a squeeze of lemon juice just before serving.

TIP: For an extra flavor kick, consider some horseradish or Tabasco sauce.

"Time to roll up my sleeves."

SAFT DRINK

This highly adaptable recipe works well with a wide combination of fruits, spices, and herbs, so use this recipe as a template. Brigitte is always looking for the next great concoction of tastes, recently favoring mint or ginger to flavor her saft. Just like in the great field of engineering, the possibilities for innovation are endless.

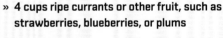

EUROPE · Brigitte

TYPE: **DRINK**

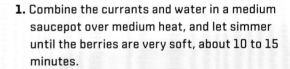

PREP TIME: 20 minutes

YIELD: Enough for several drinks

DIETARY: Gluten-Free, Vegan

» 4 cups ripe currants or other fruit, such as strawberries, blueberries, or plums

» 2 cups water

» 1½ cups sugar

» Seltzer or water, to serve

1. Combine the currants and water in a medium saucepot over medium heat, and let simmer until the berries are very soft, about 10 to 15 minutes.

2. Crush the berries and strain the juice into a clean saucepan. Add the sugar and bring back to a simmer for a minute or two, until the sugar has dissolved. Pour into a jar or bottle, and keep chilled for up to a week.

3. To serve, dilute it to taste with water or seltzer, about 6 parts water to 1 part syrup. This syrup is especially delicious in lemonade in the summer.

"There's more where that came from!"

VICHYSSOISE

Although the basement kitchen of Château Guillard was once equipped to prepare a feast for visiting diplomats and aristocrats, it was most often responsible for feeding the immediate family, and various soups were popular among the Guillards. The château is now home to just one individual, and this cold soup is more fitting than ever for Widowmaker after Talon changed her physiology to slow her heart, causing her skin to turn cold and blue.

EUROPE • *Widowmaker*

TYPE: **COMFORT**

 PREP TIME: 5 minutes
COOKING TIME: 40 minutes

 YIELD: 4 servings

 DIETARY: Gluten-Free

- » 3 tablespoons unsalted butter
- » 4 medium leeks, light green and white parts only, thinly sliced
- » 2 cloves garlic, minced
- » 1 pound potatoes, peeled and sliced
- » 4 cups chicken stock
- » 2 sprigs thyme, plus more for garnish
- » 1 sprig oregano
- » 1 bay leaf
- » ⅓ cup heavy cream, plus more for garnish
- » Salt and pepper, to taste

1. Melt the butter in a medium saucepot over medium heat, and then add the leeks and garlic. Cook, stirring occasionally, for about 10 minutes, or until the leeks are a light golden brown.

2. Add the potatoes and the chicken stock. Tie the herbs together to make a bouquet garni and add to the pot. Let this mixture simmer for about 20 minutes, or until the potatoes are completely tender.

3. Remove the bundle of herbs and discard. Purée the contents of the pot until you have a nice smooth mixture, and then stir in the heavy cream. Taste the soup, and then season to taste with salt and pepper. Serve warm or cold, garnished with a little extra thyme. Enjoy with toasted bread.

"I don't even feel the cold."

GRATIN DAUPHINOIS

This rich and savory version of scalloped potatoes is a staple in many French kitchens, often enjoyed with roast lamb in the winter. Currently, Widowmaker simply partakes of gratin dauphinois as sustenance before her next mission, but in days long gone, Amélie Lacroix used to share it with her husband, Gérard Lacroix, as it was a favorite of theirs.

EUROPE • *Widowmaker*

TYPE: *COMFORT*

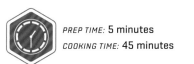

PREP TIME: 5 minutes
COOKING TIME: 45 minutes

YIELD: 4 to 6 servings

DIETARY: Gluten-Free, Vegetarian

- » 1 tablespoon unsalted butter, softened
- » 2 cups whole milk
- » 2 cups heavy cream
- » 2 cloves garlic, minced
- » 1 teaspoon savory
- » 2 pounds baking potatoes, peeled and sliced thin
- » Salt and pepper, to taste
- » Pinch of freshly grated nutmeg
- » ⅔ cup grated Gruyère cheese

1. Preheat the oven to 350°F and butter a casserole dish and set near the stove.

2. In a large saucepan over medium heat, bring the milk, cream, garlic, savory, and potatoes to a gentle simmer. Simmer for around 15 to 20 minutes, until the potatoes are very tender. Gently lift out the potatoes and transfer to the casserole dish.

3. When all the potatoes are in the dish, pour a little of the hot liquid from the simmering pan into the casserole until it covers most of the potatoes and comes about ¾ of the way up the dish.

4. Sprinkle the potatoes with salt and pepper to taste, along with the nutmeg. Spread the grated cheese over the top of everything and place in the oven.

5. Bake for 20 to 25 minutes, until bubbling and turning golden. If you'd like a more crisped top, slide the dish under the broiler for a minute or so, but keep an eye on it to prevent burning.

"Magnifique."

PAVLOVA WITH DARK FRUIT

Though this recipe for pavlova did not originate in France, Amélie Lacroix couldn't help but fall in love with the meringue-based dessert when she learned it was named for a famous ballerina, not unlike herself. Since becoming the deadly assassin Widowmaker, she feels attachment to few things. Still, she finds herself reflexively drawn to this dessert after a successful mission. A single slice is extremely rich, so—just like each of her calculated shots—one goes a long way.

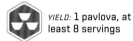

EUROPE · *Widowmaker*

TYPE: CELEBRATORY

PREP TIME: 20 minutes
BAKING AND COOLING TIME: 4 hours 30 minutes

YIELD: 1 pavlova, at least 8 servings

DIETARY: Gluten-Free, Vegetarian

MERINGUE:

» 6 large egg whites, room temperature
» Pinch of salt
» 1½ cups sugar, divided
» Dash of lemon juice
» 1 teaspoon vanilla extract
» 2 teaspoons cornstarch

CREAM TOPPING:

» 3 egg yolks
» 2 teaspoons cornstarch
» 1½ cups heavy cream
» ¼ cup sugar
» Purple food coloring
» About 4 cups of mixed fresh berries

TO MAKE THE MERINGUE:

1. Preheat the oven to 250°F and line a baking sheet with parchment paper.

2. With the egg whites in a medium-size mixing bowl, beat on medium speed until they are foamy. Add the salt and ½ cup of sugar, and then beat for about 3 minutes. Add another ½ cup of sugar, and beat for another 3 minutes. Add the remaining sugar, and this time beat until the whole mixture can hold a stiff peak and the sugar is completely dissolved. Add the remaining meringue ingredients and beat until just combined.

3. Using a large spoon, transfer the meringue to the lined baking sheet. Spread into a circle about 8 inches across, with raised edges and a slight divot in the middle to accommodate the fillings. Move to the oven and bake for 1½ hours. Once that time is up, turn off the oven and let the meringue cool in the closed oven for at least 3 hours. It's important to leave the oven door closed during this whole time.

TO MAKE THE CREAM TOPPING:

4. While the meringue is baking, you can make the topping. In a medium-size mixing bowl, beat together the egg yolks and cornstarch. Pour the heavy cream and sugar into a saucepan and bring to just under a boil over medium heat, stirring to dissolve the sugar.

5. Remove from heat and pour very slowly into the bowl of egg yolks, whisking all the while to temper the eggs. Return the whole mixture to the saucepan and place on the stove over medium-low heat. Add the food coloring and cook for an additional minute or so, until the mixture has thickened some. Pour into a clean bowl, cover with plastic, and chill for at least 1 hour.

6. When you are ready to serve, place the meringue on your serving dish. Working quickly, spread the crème pâtissière topping over it, and then heap the whole thing with beautiful fresh berries. Serve immediately.

"Let them eat cake."

115

WIDOW'S KISS

This elegant drink features dark berries and tart cherry juice. Though Widowmaker needs very little to sustain her, this drink provides a pleasant bite that she craves at the end of the day. It is best served in a tall glass and enjoyed beside the embers of a fire and the cold hiss of wind in ancestral stone halls.

EUROPE • *Widowmaker*

TYPE: *DRINK*

 PREP TIME: 5 minutes

 YIELD: 1 serving

 DIETARY: Gluten-Free, Vegan

» ¾ ounce tart cherry juice
» ¼ ounce cassis
» 3 to 4 ounces chilled champagne, to taste
» Dark berries to garnish, such as blackberries

1. Combine the cherry juice and the cassis in a champagne flute or coupe glass. Top up with champagne, and garnish with berries.

Le baiser de la veuve

"Le baiser de la veuve."

CURRYWURST

With the crisp burst of seared sausage and the richly spiced sauce, this is a robust meal for a robust soldier. Nothing prepares Reinhardt for his day like a big plate of his favorite currywurst . . . unless it's two plates of currywurst.

EUROPE • *Reinhardt*

TYPE: *PREP*

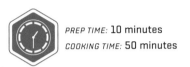
PREP TIME: 10 minutes
COOKING TIME: 50 minutes

YIELD: 2 servings

DIETARY: Gluten-Free

CURRYWURST:

» 2 to 4 bratwurst sausages
» 2 tablespoons vegetable oil, divided
» ½ medium yellow onion, diced
» 1½ cups ketchup
» ½ cup water
» Pinch of baking soda
» 1 teaspoon paprika
» 1 tablespoon curry powder, plus more for sprinkling

FRIES:

» 1½ pounds russet potatoes
» 2 to 3 tablespoons olive oil
» Sea salt

TO MAKE THE CURRYWURST:

1. Score the bratwurst on both sides in a decorative pattern. Cook the sausages in a frying pan with 1 tablespoon of oil over medium heat, with a lid on, for a couple of minutes on each side, until the sausages are golden brown and growing crisp.

2. Move the cooked sausages to a plate lined with a paper towel and keep warm. Add the rest of the oil and the onion to the pan and cook the onion a couple of minutes, until soft.

3. Add the remaining ingredients and simmer for around 5 minutes, until the mixture has thickened. Remove from heat and blend until smooth with an immersion blender.

TO MAKE THE FRIES:

4. Preheat the oven to 450°F and lightly brush a baking sheet with a little of the olive oil. Scrub the potatoes and cut into strips about ¼ inch wide. Place them in a large bowl, and then run under very hot water. Let the potatoes sit in the hot water for around 10 minutes.

5. Drain the potatoes, and then pat them so they are as dry as possible with a towel (or two). Return to the dried bowl, and add the rest of the olive oil. Spread the fries on the prepared baking sheet and sprinkle with salt. Move the baking sheet to the oven and bake for around 20 minutes. Flip the fries to ensure a more even bake, and then return to the oven for another 5 to 10 minutes.

6. Plate the sausage and fries next to each other. Then drizzle the sauce over the cooked bratwurst, and sprinkle with a little extra curry powder and serve immediately.

"Do I have time for a currywurst?"

KÄSESPÄTZLE

Käsespätzle is the ultimate German comfort food—small, soft pieces of boiled dough are coated with rich cheese, then topped with crunchy onions. It's the perfect side dish—or main course—for any meal.

Reinhardt has enjoyed this dish for many years, sometimes as a main course and sometimes alongside a juicy roast. Even now, after the Crusaders and after Overwatch, käsespätzle lifts his spirits when he's feeling a little discouraged.

EUROPE · Reinhardt

TYPE: COMFORT

SPÄTZLE:

» 2 cups all-purpose flour

» 4 eggs

» 1 teaspoon salt, plus more for boiling

» ½ cup water

SAUCE:

» 7 ounces grated Emmentaler or cheddar cheese

» 4 tablespoons unsalted butter

» 1 medium yellow onion, chopped fine

» Dash of light brown sugar

» Parsley to garnish

PREP TIME: 5 minutes
SETTING TIME: 1 hour
COOKING TIME: 30 minutes

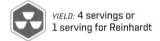

YIELD: 4 servings or 1 serving for Reinhardt

DIETARY: Vegetarian

TO MAKE THE SPÄTZLE:

1. Combine the flour, eggs, salt, and water in a medium-size mixing bowl. Beat together with a hand mixer until you have a smooth dough that is sticky but not too dense. You're aiming for a consistency that is just loose enough to be pressed through a spätzle press or a colander. Cover the dough and let sit for 1 hour to let the gluten develop.

2. When you're ready to make the spätzle, preheat the oven to 400°F and butter a large baking dish. Bring a large pot of water to a boil, adding a dash of salt. Working with a large spoonful at a time, either press the dough through a spätzle press or scrape through the holes of a colander into the boiling water. The dumplings are done when they float to the surface. Fish out the spätzle and transfer them to a large mixing bowl.

TO ASSEMBLE:

3. Once all the spätzle are cooked, layer them in your prepared baking dish, alternating spätzle with the cheese, ending with a layer of cheese. Bake for about 15 minutes, until the cheese is melted and starting to turn golden.

4. While the spätzle bake, make the caramelized onions. Melt the butter in a medium saucepan over medium-low heat and add the onions. Cook until soft, and then add the brown sugar. Continue to cook until the onions are brown and fragrant. Remove from heat.

5. When the initial bake of the käsespätzle is done, remove from oven, top with the caramelized onions, and return to the oven for another 5 to 10 minutes. To serve, sprinkle with chopped parsley.

"Bring me another!"

EICHENWALDE CAKE

Traditional Black Forest cake pairs cherry and chocolate, but Eichenwalde—the abandoned town in the middle of the Black Forest—is known for its berries. Rich chocolate cake, fluffy frosting, and fresh, juicy berries combine for a gorgeous dessert. Though Eichenwalde holds hard memories for Reinhardt after he lost Balderich von Adler in battle there, this cake helps him remember and cherish everything he learned from his mentor.

EUROPE • *Reinhardt*

TYPE: *CELEBRATORY*

PREP TIME: 15 minutes
BAKING TIME: 25 minutes

YIELD: 1 cake, at least 8 large servings

DIETARY: Vegetarian

CAKE:

» 2 cups all-purpose flour

» 1 cup unsweetened cocoa powder

» 2 teaspoons baking powder

» 1 teaspoon baking soda

» 1 teaspoon salt

» ½ cup (1 stick) unsalted butter, softened

» 1 cup sugar

» 2 eggs

» 1 teaspoon vanilla extract

» 1½ cups whole milk

» ½ cup boiling water

FROSTING:

» 2½ cups heavy cream

» 1 teaspoon vanilla extract

» ¼ cup powdered sugar

» ¼ cup unsweetened cocoa powder

» 2 pints fresh mixed berries

» Fresh mint, to garnish

1. Preheat the oven to 350°F and lightly butter and flour two 8-inch round cake pans. In a small bowl, mix together the flour, cocoa powder, baking powder, baking soda, and salt, and then set aside.

2. In a large mixing bowl, cream together the butter and sugar, and then mix in the eggs and vanilla until you have a nice smooth batter. Add the milk and the flour mixture in alternating batches. Finally, whisk in the boiling water until just mixed. Divide the batter between the two baking pans and bake for around 25 minutes, or until a toothpick inserted into the middle of the cake comes out clean. Remove the cakes from the oven and let cool completely before turning out of the pans.

3. Once the cakes are cool, mix the frosting. Combine the heavy cream, vanilla, sugar, and cocoa powder in a large bowl, and then beat with an electric mixer for a couple of minutes, or until stiff peaks form.

4. To assemble the cake, place one of the cooled cake rounds on your serving dish. Spread a thin layer of the frosting over the top of it, and then arrange a layer of fresh berries over it. Spread another thin layer of frosting on the bottom of the second cake, and then gently place this on top of the first. Spread or pipe the rest of the frosting over the top of the cake, and then stud with remaining berries and mint leaves, to garnish. Serve straightaway.

"Precision German engineering."

ALTBIERBOWLE

Beneath Reinhardt's suit of armor is a jovial man with an insatiable zest for life. This jolly modern-day knight can hold the attention of a crowd, especially when he has a pint of altbierbowle in hand. The fruit flavors and the sweet syrup blend surprisingly well with the dark beer, making a great drink for summer weather and garden parties.

EUROPE • *Reinhardt*

TYPE: *DRINK*

PREP TIME: 5 minutes
COOKING TIME: 5 minutes
STEEPING TIME: 2 hours or overnight

YIELD: 2 servings

DIETARY: Vegan

» ¼ cup sugar

» ¼ cup water

» 1 apple, cored and diced

» ½ cup sliced strawberries

» ½ cup raspberries

» 2 pints chilled German altbier (amber ale or creamy stout can substitute)

» Mint and berries to garnish

1. Combine the sugar and water in a small saucepan over medium heat, swirling occasionally until the sugar has dissolved. Remove from heat and allow to cool slightly. Place the apple, strawberries, and raspberries in a bowl, and pour the sugar syrup over them. Let this sit for about 2 hours, or overnight for stronger flavor.

2. To serve, divide the fruit and syrup between two pint glasses (or one stein for Reinhardt) and pour the beer over them. Garnish, and enjoy!

TIP: For a gluten-free version, use a gluten-free beer or a hard cider.

"Prost!"

BIRD-SHAPED PRETZELS

Sadly, pretzels don't transform into assault-cannon mode when battlefield conditions change. But, luckily, they do come in all sorts of interesting shapes.

Though Bastion avoids humans, its innocent curiosity can get the better of it sometimes. Bastion discovered these pretzels being made in a small town on the edge of the Black Forest where the residents have been forming them in the shape of birds for generations.

EUROPE • Bastion

TYPE: COMFORT

PREP AND COOKING TIME:
50 minutes
RISING TIME: 1 hour
BAKING TIME: 12 to 15 minutes

YIELD: 8 pretzels

DIETARY: Vegetarian

» 6½ cups warm water, divided

» 2 tablespoons packed light brown sugar

» ½ teaspoon salt, plus more for sprinkling

» 2 teaspoons instant yeast

» 3 tablespoons unsalted butter, melted

» 4 cups all-purpose flour

» ⅓ cup baking soda

» ½ teaspoon coriander (optional)

» ½ teaspoon fennel seeds (optional)

» Dried currants for eyes

» Slivered almonds for beaks

1. In a large mixing bowl, combine 1½ cups of warm water, brown sugar, salt, yeast, and butter. Gradually add the flour a cup at a time until the dough pulls away from the sides of the bowl.

2. Turn out onto a lightly floured surface and knead for a few minutes, until the dough bounces back when poked. Lightly grease the bowl and return the dough to it. Cover lightly with plastic wrap and allow to rise in a warm place for 1 hour, or until roughly doubled in size.

3. Once the dough has risen, preheat the oven to 400°F, and set out a baking sheet lined with parchment paper. Add the remaining 5 cups of warm water and baking soda to a medium saucepan and bring to a simmer. Punch the dough back down and divide into 8 equal pieces. Roll each piece of dough into a rope about 10 inches long, and then tie into a knot.

4. Flatten one end of the knot for the tail, score with scissors or a knife, and leave the other as the head. Repeat this with the remaining dough. Once your water is simmering, gently slide one or two birds into the water at a time. Let them cook for about a minute each, spooning hot water over them, until they are puffy. Transfer the finished birds to the baking sheet.

5. When all the pretzels have been boiled, season with a sprinkle of salt, coriander, and fennel if using, and then use a small knife to make holes in the dough for the currant eyes and almond beaks. Insert the currants and almonds, and then bake the pretzels for 12 to 15 minutes, until golden brown.

"ZWOO BEEP BOOP BEEP."

TREATS FOR WILD BIRDS

When human interaction gets a little fraught with conflict, many of us humans like to escape to the forest. That's Bastion's daily life. After all, birds didn't program robots for destruction and then turn around and try to destroy *them*.

Life can be hard for wild birds in winter when food is scarce. Because Ganymede's nest-building skills leave something to be desired, Bastion lets its little friend travel with it. Make your own feathered friends by creating this decorative edible ornament and hanging it where you can watch all types of birds enjoy.

EUROPE • *Bastion*

TYPE: *NONE*

» **4 tablespoons unflavored gelatin**

» **1 cup boiling water**

» **3 tablespoons creamy nut butter**

» **4 cups premixed birdseed**

PREP TIME: 20 minutes
SETTING TIME: Overnight

YIELD: About 10 ornaments

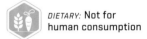
DIETARY: Not for human consumption

1. Line a baking sheet with parchment paper and set approximately 10 cookie cutters on it. Cut several straws into pieces a few inches in length, and set aside.

2. Pour the gelatin into a large mixing bowl, and then pour the boiling water over it and stir until dissolved. Stir in the nut butter until that, too, has dissolved. Finally, stir in the birdseed, making sure that the whole bowl is evenly mixed. If the mixture is still too wet to form, let it sit for a few minutes.

3. Spoon the mix into cookie cutters, pressing down to make sure each shape is completely filled. Repeat until you have used up all the birdseed. Gently press a piece of straw into the seed mix near the top of the cookie cutter to form a hole. You can leave the straw in, or remove it. Put in refrigerator and let the ornaments chill overnight. To hang, remove the straw from each shape and gently press the ornament out of the cookie cutter. Thread a piece of twine through the hole, knot, and hang outdoors for the wild birds to enjoy.

"BEEP."

BIRCHER MUESLI

Mercy may have many lifesaving tricks of her own, but she can definitely appreciate another healer's methods. This delicately flavored Swiss oatmeal is named for the early-twentieth-century doctor who sought to heal his patients with a diet focused on raw food. Given its healthy origins, it's no wonder that Mercy chooses this recipe to start her mornings and recommends it to her patients. Rumor has it that even Genji learned to like it, after a time.

Both healthy and rich in tradition, Bircher muesli has a slight tartness from the apple cider vinegar that balances the creamy sweetness of the oats. Nuts and apples provide a little textural variation, bringing the whole meal together.

EUROPE • *Mercy*

TYPE: *PREP*

- 4 tablespoons rolled oats
- 6 tablespoons water
- 1 apple, cored and grated
- 1 tablespoon apple cider vinegar
- 1 tablespoon sweetened condensed milk
- Assorted toppings, such as almonds, hazelnuts, and fresh or dried fruit

SOAKING TIME: At least 8 hours or overnight

COOKING TIME: 5 minutes (optional)

YIELD: 2 servings

DIETARY: Gluten-Free, Vegetarian

1. Combine the oats, water, apple, and apple cider vinegar in a small bowl. Cover and let sit overnight, or at least 8 hours.

2. To serve, stir in the condensed milk and add any additional toppings. The muesli can be eaten at room temperature or warmed before serving.

"Take two, and call me in the morning."

BASLER BRUNSLI

These flavorful cookies originated in Basel, Switzerland, in the 1700s and have been a traditional staple in Swiss kitchens ever since. Especially popular at holiday time, these soft morsels are bursting with spices and rich almond flavor.

The Swiss can't resist their country's chocolate—plus, as many tricks as Mercy has up her sleeve, she knows that sometimes the best remedies are the simplest. The joy that a cookie brings can heal all manner of ailments.

PREP TIME: 10 minutes
CHILLING TIME: 2 hours
DRYING TIME: 3 hours
BAKING TIME: About 15 minutes

YIELD: About 2 dozen

DIETARY: Gluten-Free, Vegetarian

- ¾ cup almond flour
- ½ cup sugar
- 3 ounces semisweet chocolate chips
- 1 teaspoon ground cinnamon
- Pinch of ground cloves
- 1 egg white, beaten
- Granulated sugar for dusting

1. Pulse the almond flour, sugar, chocolate chips, and spices in a food processor until the chocolate is finely ground. Add the egg white and pulse a few more times. If needed, add a little more almond flour until the dough comes together into one lump. Wrap the dough in plastic and chill for at least 2 hours, or overnight.

2. When you are ready to shape the cookies, line a baking sheet with parchment paper. Roll out the chilled dough between two sheets of parchment paper, dusting with a little extra sugar if it is too sticky. Roll to about ¼ inch thick, and then cut into your desired shapes. Transfer these to the parchment-lined baking sheet. Let these cookies sit for at least 3 hours to allow the tops to dry out, or place in the refrigerator overnight.

3. Preheat the oven to 300°F and bake for about 15 minutes, until the cookies are a little puffy. Let the cookies cool for about 5 minutes before moving them to a wire rack to finish cooling.

"I got you some chocolate cookies. Swiss, they're the best!"

ALPINE CHEESE SOUP

Also known as *soupe de chalet*, this hearty, warming soup originated in the mountains of western Switzerland. It is easy to prepare, packed with vegetables and nutrients, and deliciously cheesy. A good physician knows better than to pour from an empty cup, so Mercy has been known to treat herself to a cozy bowl when she is feeling spent.

EUROPE · *Mercy*

TYPE: *COMFORT*

- » 1 tablespoon unsalted butter
- » 1 large leek, white parts only, diced
- » 2 large carrots, finely diced
- » 2 cups vegetable stock
- » 1 cup whole milk
- » 1 white potato, peeled and diced large
- » ½ cup fresh spinach, sliced thin
- » 2 cups grated Emmentaler or Gruyère cheese
- » ¼ cup heavy cream
- » Salt and pepper, to taste

 PREP TIME: 30 minutes

 YIELD: 4 servings

 DIETARY: Gluten-Free, Vegetarian

1. In a medium saucepan, melt the butter over medium heat. Add the leek and carrots and cook for a few minutes, until the leeks are soft. Add the vegetable stock, milk, and potatoes; cover the pot; and simmer for another 20 minutes or so, until the vegetables are all cooked through and fork tender.

2. Uncover the pot and stir in the spinach for about a minute or so, and then gradually stir in the cheese, adding more as it melts. Finish with a splash of heavy cream, and then season to taste with salt and pepper.

"Helping those in need is its own reward."

VALKYRIE'S FLIGHT

With flowers grown on the Alpine slopes, honey from local bees, and a little dash of something strong, this recipe will warm you from the inside out and improve your immune system in the long run. Unlike its caffeinated English counterpart that uses black tea, this toddy employs soothing chamomile to encourage rest.

Dr. Ziegler, like many who care for others, knows the healing value of a good cup of tea, for the soul as much as for the body—especially beneficial with that nip of brandy to relax your nerves after a life-threatening ordeal.

EUROPE • *Mercy*

TYPE: *DRINK*

 PREP TIME: 5 minutes

 YIELD: 1 serving

 DIETARY: Gluten-Free, Vegetarian

- » 1 chamomile tea bag
- » 1½ cups boiling water
- » Honey, to taste
- » 1 ounce elderflower liqueur
- » 1 ounce brandy
- » Dash of fresh lemon juice
- » Lemon peel to garnish

1. Put the tea bag in a mug and pour the boiling water over. Stir in the honey and let steep for about 5 minutes.

2. Remove the tea bag, and add the elderflower liqueur, brandy, and lemon juice. Garnish with a piece of lemon peel, and let the healing begin.

TIP: Feel free to omit the liquor for a nonalcoholic version.

"Valkyrie online."

AUSTRALIA

JUNKERTOWN LOADED BURGER

While the best way to make this recipe is over a piping-hot barbeque, this stovetop version is suited to all places and all seasons.

    This burger's as loaded up as a booby-trapped hover-barge. Junkrat's mind is a little . . . scattered these days, so when it comes to choosing toppings? Forget about it. He just puts a little of everything he's got on that bun and calls it a day. Roadhog took care to write down his compatriot's favorite amalgamation—in the unlikely event they end up with these exact ingredients again.

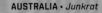

AUSTRALIA • *Junkrat*

TYPE: *PREP*

BURGER:

» 12 ounces ground beef

» 1 teaspoon crushed red chili flakes

» 1 clove garlic, minced

» Salt, to taste

» 2 slices cheddar cheese

» 2 tablespoons unsalted butter

» 2 canned pineapple rings

» 2 slices red onion, separated into rings

» 2 eggs

TOPPINGS:

» 2 hamburger buns, toasted

» 2 leaves lettuce

» 2 slices tomato

» 4 slices pickled beets

» 4 slices cooked bacon

PREP TIME: 5 minutes
COOKING TIME: 15 minutes

YIELD: 2 burgers

DIETARY: None

1. In a medium bowl, combine the ground beef, chili flakes, and garlic, and then form into two patties. Sprinkle liberally with salt.

2. Bring a frying pan to medium-high heat. Once the pan is hot, add the burgers, letting them sear on one side for about 3 to 5 minutes, depending on your preferences, and then flipping over for another 3 to 5 minutes. Top each burger with a slice of cheddar cheese, remove from the pan, and keep warm while you prepare the rest of the toppings.

3. Turn the heat down to medium, and then add the butter to the same pan. Sear the pineapple rings for a minute or so, until brown. Set aside. Add the onion rings to the pan and cook for several minutes, until soft. Set these aside too. Finally, fry the eggs in the pan until the yolks are just set, around 3 minutes.

4. To assemble the burgers, start with the bun and add a layer of lettuce and tomato, then beets and pineapple, then the burger patty, bacon, and top with the fried egg.

"Revenge is a dish best served flaming hot!"

CHOCOLATE CRACKLE BOMBS

If you like chocolate, fun desserts, and explosions of questionable safety, then these bombs are for you. Nothing sets off a good celebration like some fireworks. Explosions of crackly flavor, the sharp bite of licorice—what's not to love? Junkrat can scavenge any number of delicious ingredients to make variations on these tasty flavors bombs. The recipe below is his go-to combination.

AUSTRALIA • *Junkrat*

TYPE: *CELEBRATORY*

» ½ cup peanut or other nut butter

» ⅓ cup honey

» ¼ cup cocoa powder, plus extra for dusting

» 1 teaspoon vanilla extract

» Pinch of salt

» 2 cups puffed rice

» ½ cup coconut flakes (optional)

» 2 ounces chocolate chips

» Several pieces of round licorice, some thin and some thick

 PREP TIME: 25 minutes

 YIELD: About a dozen

 DIETARY: Gluten-Free, Vegetarian

1. In a medium mixing bowl, combine the nut butter and honey. Stir in the cocoa powder, vanilla, and salt, beating until smooth. Finally, stir in the puffed rice and coconut flakes, if using. Place in the fridge to chill for about 15 minutes. Once chilled, form into balls of about 2 tablespoons each, and place back in the fridge.

2. To assemble the bombs, slice the thin licorice into strips about an inch long for the fuses, and set aside. Slice the larger licorice into chunks about ½ inch long to make the fuse casing, and poke a hole in one end with a knife. Insert the fuse into the hole, and repeat with as many fuses as you have crackle balls.

3. In a heatproof bowl, melt the chocolate chips in the microwave (a small saucepan on the stovetop also works) in 30-second bursts, stirring occasionally until you have a smooth melted consistency. Remove the balls from the fridge and set nearby. Dip half the fuse casing into the melted chocolate, then press onto the top of a crackle ball. The chocolate should set in a few seconds. Repeat with all the remaining bombs, then plate to serve.

"If you can't handle the heat, stay out of the kitchen!"

BOBAS AWAY

Does anything delight quite like the sweet chewiness of boba pearls? Settled down at the bottom of a delicious cup of tea sweetened to taste, they're like finding treasure.

A fan of all sorts of treasure, Junkrat keeps a steady supply of half-sweet tea with boba in his canteen. It keeps him energized, whether he's planning his next ambitious heist or building explosives just for the joy of watching something blow up.

AUSTRALIA • *Junkrat*

TYPE: *DRINK*

PREP TIME: 20 minutes
CHILLING TIME: 30 minutes

YIELD: 1 serving

DIETARY: Gluten-Free, Vegetarian

» ¼ cup uncooked tapioca boba pearls
» ¼ cup honey
» 1 to 2 bags strong black tea
» 2 cups boiling water
» Sweetened condensed milk

1. Prepare the boba according to their package directions, and then soak in honey. Set aside.

2. Brew a strong cup of tea with one or two tea bags, steeping for about 5 minutes, and then remove the tea bags and chill the tea in the refrigerator for at least 30 minutes.

3. To prepare the drink, pour the boba into a pint glass or other tall glass. Pour the tea over, and then sweeten to taste with condensed milk.

*"Come on come on come on!
I. Hate. Waiting."*

POPCORN SNACK MIX

Mako Rutledge may have lost his humanity, but he hasn't lost his appetite. And since life on the road as part of an international criminal duo doesn't always lend itself to regular meals, snacks are good to have handy.

Crunchy, salty, nutty, and sweet, this snack mix is hard to put down once you start munching. The coating of caramel over several crunchy ingredients is a match made in heaven. Sort of like Roadhog and Junkrat . . . just with more flavor and less total mayhem.

AUSTRALIA · *Roadhog*

TYPE: *COMFORT*

» About 6 to 8 cups plain popcorn

» 3 cups Rice Chex cereal

» 1½ cups small twist pretzels

» ¼ cup slivered almonds

» 6 tablespoons unsalted butter

» 1 cup packed light brown sugar

» ¼ cup light corn syrup or honey

» 1 cup or more peanut butter or chocolate candies

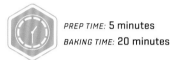

PREP TIME: 5 minutes
BAKING TIME: 20 minutes

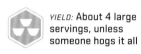

YIELD: About 4 large servings, unless someone hogs it all

DIETARY: Gluten-Free, Vegetarian

1. Preheat the oven to 300°F and lightly butter a large rimmed baking sheet. In a large mixing bowl, combine the popcorn, cereal, pretzels, and almonds, stirring to combine. Spread these over the baking sheet and set aside.

2. In a small saucepan, melt the butter, and then add the brown sugar and corn syrup or honey. Cook over medium-high heat until bubbling. Continue to cook for a few minutes, while stirring, until the ingredients come together and thicken somewhat. Remove from heat and drizzle over the popcorn mixture with a spoon.

3. Move the baking sheet to the oven and bake for around 10 minutes, and then take out of the oven, toss with a spatula to help cover all the pieces with the caramel, and return to the oven for another 10 minutes. When done, remove from oven and allow to cool for a few minutes, until cool enough to touch. Break apart the popcorn mixture into a large mixing bowl, and then add the candy once completely cool.

"Pure hogpower."

FAIRY BREAD

Although this might seem like a deceptively simple recipe, no birthday party from Sydney to the rugged outback would be complete without a heaping plate of fairy bread. The creamy butter, soft bread, and explosion of sprinkles all combine to make a unique and happy dish.

These delicate little slices of bread remind Roadhog of a better time, when he could run his farm in peace and had few cares in the world. It takes a lot of scrap to trade for fresh bread and sprinkles, but he'll make the effort from time to time when the road ahead feels dark.

AUSTRALIA · *Roadhog*

TYPE: *CELEBRATORY*

» 4 slices white bread

» 3 tablespoons unsalted butter, room temperature

» ½ cup round sprinkles (also known as 100s and 1000s, or nonpareils)

 PREP TIME: 5 minutes

 YIELD: 1 to 4 servings, if you're sharing

DIETARY: Vegetarian

1. Carefully trim the crusts off each slice of bread. Spread a thick layer of butter over each slice, and then shake the sprinkles on top, pressing down gently to make sure they stick. Slice bread into triangles and serve.

"I'm going hog wild!"

"RADIOACTIVE" SODA FLOAT

When the sun is high over the outback and the heat is just too much to bear, sometimes you need a little pick-me-up. The refreshing fizz and cold citrus of this soda float make it the most satisfying treat in the scrapyard. This little beauty was thought up by the proprietor of the take-away food joint just inside the gates of Junkertown, and Mako discovered it one day after successfully selling off his scrap metal. He now drops in whenever he can—that is, if he can get back in through the gates without the Queen of Junkertown noticing.

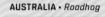

AUSTRALIA · Roadhog

TYPE: **DRINK**

 PREP TIME: 5 minutes

 YIELD: 1 serving

 DIETARY: Gluten-Free, Vegetarian

» A few drops of angostura bitters
» Lemon, lime, or orange sherbet
» 12 ounces lemon-lime soda

1. Add a few drops of angostura bitters to the bottom of a pint glass. Add 3 to 4 scoops of sherbet, and then pour in the lemon-lime soda, pausing to let the foam subside, then topping up with more soda.

   TIP: To help the drink last longer, scoop balls of sherbet onto a baking sheet lined with parchment paper and refreeze for at least 2 hours, or overnight.

"Welcome to the apocalypse."

ASIA

RIKIMARU RAMEN

Although nothing can beat the generations of expertise found amid the piping-hot pots of ramen from a good restaurant, this at-home version is a great stand-in when you can't get the real thing. With nourishing pieces of roasted chicken and plenty of noodles, this is a perfect feel-better dish for cold weather and blue days.

ASIA • *Genji*

TYPE: *PREP*

No restaurant was more popular with the young Shimada brothers than the Rikimaru Ramen shop just outside the gates of their family compound. They share fond memories of trying to outeat each other and seeing who could eat the spiciest bowl. The loss of those happy days weighs heavily on Genji, but he has made his peace with the events of the past and looks to a more hopeful future. Perhaps one day that future will include his brother, Hanzo, and a steaming bowl of ramen.

 PREP TIME: 10 minutes
COOKING TIME: 35 minutes

 YIELD: 2 servings

 DIETARY: None

» 2 chicken breasts (boneless, skin-on)

» Salt and pepper, to season

» 1 tablespoon unsalted butter

» 2 teaspoons sesame oil

» 2 teaspoons fresh ginger, minced

» 3 teaspoons fresh garlic, minced

» 2 tablespoons soy sauce

» 2 tablespoons mirin

» 4 cups chicken stock

» ½ cup fresh shitake mushrooms, sliced

» 1 to 2 teaspoons fine sea salt, to taste

» 2 eggs

» ½ cup scallions, sliced

» Two 3-ounce packs dried ramen noodles

1. Preheat the oven to 375°F and set aside a small baking sheet. Sprinkle the chicken breasts with salt and pepper, and then melt the butter in a medium frying pan. Cook the chicken, skin side down, for around 5 minutes, until the skin is golden. Flip and cook for another 5 minutes, and then transfer the chicken to the baking sheet.

2. Move to the oven and cook for around 15 minutes, until cooked through. Remove from the oven and keep warm while you make the rest of the dish.

3. While the chicken is cooking, heat the oil in a medium saucepan. Add the ginger and garlic and cook for a minute or two, until soft and fragrant. Add the soy sauce and mirin, cook for a minute, then add the stock. Simmer for around 5 minutes, and then add the mushrooms and sea salt. Simmer for another 10 minutes.

4. While the broth is cooking, make your soft-boiled eggs. In a small saucepan, bring 1 inch of water to a simmer. Add the eggs, cover, and cook for about 6 minutes. Immediately transfer the eggs to a bowl of ice water to stop them from cooking further. When they have cooled, peel and set aside until you are ready to assemble the ramen. When the eggs are done, add more water to the pot and cook the noodles until soft, about 2 to 3 minutes.

5. Once the broth is done, divide the noodles between two serving bowls. Slice the chicken breast thinly, and then add one sliced breast to each bowl. Add the scallions, and then slice the boiled eggs in half and add one egg to each bowl. Serve straightaway.

"Kaedama!"

SOBA-CHA CUSTARD

A new take on traditional buckwheat tea, this dessert has the same distinctive nutty, earthy flavor. It was invented by the Shimada family's chef as a way of rewarding Genji and Hanzo for studying. Genji used to eat his looking out over the rest of Hanamura with his legs dangling over the ledge of the roof of the Shimadas' ancestral home.

ASIA · Genji

TYPE: COMFORT

» 1½ cups heavy cream

» ¼ cup sugar

» ⅛ cup soba-cha, or roasted-buckwheat tea

» 2 eggs

PREP TIME: 15 minutes
CHILLING TIME: 1 hour

YIELD: 1 to 2 servings

DIETARY: Gluten-Free, Vegetarian

1. In a small saucepan, bring the cream and sugar to just under a simmer, stirring until the sugar has dissolved. Add the soba-cha and let steep for around 5 minutes, until fragrant.

2. Crack the eggs into a small bowl. While whisking steadily, pour the cream mixture into the bowl with the eggs to temper them. Strain this mixture back into a clean saucepan, and then cook over medium-low heat for a couple of minutes while whisking, until thickened somewhat. Remove from heat and pour into a serving bowl.

3. Lay a piece of plastic wrap directly on the custard and chill for at least 1 hour before serving.

"A warrior's reward."

GREEN DRAGON TEA

Genji developed this drink himself using some of his favorite flavors from home. Along with meditation, it helped sustain him during some of the colder nights in his time at the Shambali Monastery in Nepal with Zenyatta.

ASIA • *Genji*

TYPE: **DRINK**

 PREP TIME: 10 minutes

 YIELD: 1 serving

 DIETARY: Gluten-Free, Vegan

» 1 cup water
» 1 green tea bag
» 1 inch fresh ginger root, sliced thin
» Several slices of cucumber
» ½ teaspoon sugar, or more to taste
» 2 ounces sake
» 1 ounce orange liqueur

1. Combine the water, green tea bag, ginger, cucumber, and sugar in a small saucepan. Bring to just under a simmer, and then remove from heat and let sit for around 5 minutes.

2. Add the sake and orange liqueur and bring back to just under a simmer before removing from heat again. Strain into a heatproof glass or mug and enjoy hot.

TIP: This drink is pleasant served warm, but if you are using higher-quality sake, try it chilled, as more of the individual flavors will come through.

"I need tea!"

TAMAGO KAKE GOHAN

Hanzo grew up surrounded by wealth and servants, and could have had anything he wanted. But after the clan forced him to kill his brother, he rejected his birthright and now travels the world, living a simple life and perfecting his skills. The heir apparent of the powerful Shimada clan would never have eaten such a simplistic meal as tamago kake gohan. But now, Hanzo revels in its simplicity as he continues his journey toward atonement.

ASIA • *Hanzo*

TYPE: *PREP*

- 1 cup uncooked white rice
- 2 cups water
- ½ teaspoon soy sauce
- Pinch of salt
- Splash of mirin
- 1 egg, plus 1 optional egg yolk
- Furikake seasoning (optional)

 COOKING TIME: 25 minutes

 *YIELD:* 1 serving, plus extra rice

 DIETARY: Vegetarian

1. Rinse the rice several times in cold water, draining off between rinses. Then place the rice in a medium saucepan and add the water. Cover and place over high heat and bring to a boil, which should take about 3 to 5 minutes. Immediately turn down to low heat and let cook for about 5 to 10 minutes more with the lid on. When you start to hear the hissing and cracking that indicates the water has been absorbed, remove from heat. Let sit, covered, for about 10 more minutes.

2. While the rice is still piping hot, transfer half of it into a bowl and quickly whisk in the soy sauce, salt, mirin, and whole raw egg. Beat together for a minute or to, until the mixture is gooey and thickened. Sprinkle with furikake seasoning, and if you'd like, top with an extra egg yolk, then serve.

"The dragon hungers."

SHIMADA TEMPURA

In Hanzo's younger days, he would walk the streets of Hanamura, diligently completing the tasks his father had set out before him. If his responsibilities were handled early, he would treat himself to a helping of tempura vegetables and shrimp from one of the numerous stalls that dot the city. After the deadly conflict with his brother, Genji, Hanzo became sterner and more distant. But sometimes the smell and taste of tempura bring him back to a simpler time and he relaxes, if just for a moment.

ASIA · *Hanzo*

TYPE: **COMFORT**

BATTER:

» 2 cups all-purpose flour

» 1 egg, cold

» 1 cup cold water

FOR FRYING:

» Vegetable oil for frying

» ½ small eggplant, skinned and cubed

» 1 cup enoki mushrooms

» 1 small carrot, skinned and julienned

» ½ cup water chestnut slices

» 12 tail-less shrimp

 PREP TIME: 5 minutes
FRYING TIME: 20 minutes

 YIELD: 2 to 4 servings

 DIETARY: None

1. Bring several inches of oil to around 350°F in a tall saucepan.

2. While the oil is heating, quickly make up your batter. Combine the flour and egg, then the water, stirring as little as possible until just mixed. It's important to keep the batter cold!

3. To fry, dip the vegetables into the batter, and then lower them into the hot oil. They should sink to the bottom before almost immediately popping back to the top. Fry only a few pieces at a time to ensure that the oil stays hot enough.

4. Fry the vegetables first, and then follow with any seafood. Fry everything for a couple of minutes, turning occasionally, until a nice golden brown. Remove to a plate lined with paper towels to drain. Serve hot.

"Have a taste of this."

SAKURA MOCHI

In the spring, Hanamura is bursting with the beautiful pink blossoms of sakura trees. Hanzo used to enjoy these pink treats as a child during *hanami*—the collective viewing of the cherry blossoms that occurs every spring.

Soft and sweet with a flavor distinct to the sakura leaves, these mochi require a little bit of muscle to make, but the end result is worth the effort.

ASIA • *Hanzo*

TYPE: *CELEBRATORY*

SOAKING TIME: 1 hour minimum
COOKING TIME: 50 minutes
RESTING TIME: 1 hour

YIELD: 6 mochi

DIETARY: Gluten-Free, Vegetarian

» ¾ cup sweet glutinous rice

» ¾ cup water

» 1 tablespoon sugar

» 1 drop red food coloring

» 3 tablespoons red bean paste

» 6 pickled sakura leaves

1. Begin by rinsing the rice in a small bowl several times in warm water, and then cover with water and let soak for at least 1 hour, or overnight. Likewise soak the sakura leaves in water for around 15 minutes, and then pat dry.

2. Once the rice is done soaking, drain the excess water and add the ¾ cup water to the bowl. Stir in the sugar and red food coloring—you're aiming for a light pink color, so be careful not to add too much.

3. Cover the bowl with plastic and microwave for about 5 minutes, stirring once at the midway point, taking care to avoid the steam. When done, leave covered for 5 more minutes to allow the rice to keep cooking. Alternatively, you can cook the rice according to the directions on its packaging.

4. Once the rice is cooked, mash it together either with a mortar and pestle or the flat of a spoon until nearly smooth and very sticky. Divide the rice into 6 equal portions. Likewise divide the bean paste into 6 equal pieces.

5. Using dampened fingers, gently press one portion of the sticky rice into a flat disc on a small piece of plastic wrap. Place a ball of bean paste in the middle, and then fold the rice around to completely cover the paste. Fold the plastic around the rice ball and twist tightly to compress the rice. Unwrap the mochi and wrap with a sakura leaf. Let each mochi sit for around 1 hour to absorb the flavor from the leaf, and then enjoy the same day.

"True mastery is the highest art."

MEKA KIMBAP

It's no secret that D.Va is a fan of flavorful and portable food, and there's no food more tasty and mobile than kimbap: cooked rice and various fillings all rolled up in a sheet of dried seaweed.

D.Va may love chips and Nano Cola, but once fans got wind of D.Va's favorite kimbap fillings—including meat, egg, kimchi, and avocado—this MEKA kimbap became all the rage in Busan.

ASIA • *D.Va*

TYPE: *PREP*

 PREP TIME: 20 minutes
COOKING TIME: 10 minutes

 YIELD: 4 rolls

 DIETARY: None

- » 2 teaspoons soy sauce
- » 1 teaspoon rice wine
- » 1 teaspoon sugar
- » 1 teaspoon sesame oil
- » ½ teaspoon minced garlic
- » ½ pound stir-fry beef, cut into long strips
- » 1 egg, beaten
- » 4 cups cooked short grain sushi rice, cooled
- » 4 sheets nori sushi seaweed
- » ½ cup kimchi, finely cut
- » 1 avocado, thinly sliced

1. In a medium frying pan, combine the soy sauce, rice wine, sugar, sesame oil, and garlic over medium heat. When the mixture is hot and sizzling, add the beef and cook for several minutes, turning occasionally until cooked all the way through.

2. Remove from heat and allow to cool. Clean out the pan, and then pour the beaten egg into a long strip down the middle of the pan. Cook for a minute or so, and then flip to cook the other side. Remove the egg to a clean plate and cut into strips no bigger than ½ inch wide.

3. To assemble the kimbap, spread a quarter of the cooked rice over a sheet of nori, pressing down to make a dense layer of rice. On one edge of this, lay out a strip of the cooked beef, egg, a quarter of the kimchi, and a quarter of the avocado. Starting at the end with all of the ingredients, carefully but firmly begin rolling up the nori, rice, and fillings until you have rolled the whole roll up. If the seaweed isn't sticking to the far end, use a few dabs of water or a few grains of cooked rice to seal the seaweed together. Place the roll on a cutting board, seam side down. Using a very sharp knife, cut into slices roughly 1 inch wide. Repeat with all the remaining ingredients.

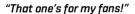

"That one's for my fans!"

JAPCHAE

D.Va and Dae-hyun have spent countless hours working together on the mechs that help keep Korea safe. When critical repairs pile up after a particularly tough battle, the two don't have much time to stop and eat, so they eat a lot of instant noodles. Every once in a while, though, D.Va will finally take a break and sit down to eat a warm plate of Dae-hyun's japchae, featuring lots of fresh vegetables and the strong nutty flavor of sesame.

ASIA · D.Va

TYPE: *COMFORT*

 PREP TIME: 20 minutes
COOKING TIME: 20 minutes

 YIELD: 4 to 6 servings

 DIETARY: None

JAPCHAE:

» 6 ounces Korean potato starch noodles

» Handful fresh spinach, julienned

» Vegetable oil for stir-frying

» 1 carrot, julienned

» 2 shallots, thinly sliced

» 2 scallions, julienned

» Handful shiitake mushrooms, thinly sliced

» 4 ounces stir-fry beef, cut into bite-size pieces

SAUCE:

» ¼ cup soy sauce

» 2½ tablespoons sugar

» 2 tablespoons sesame oil

» 1 to 2 cloves garlic, minced

» 2 teaspoons sesame seeds

» Salt and pepper, to taste

1. Bring a medium pot of water to a boil and cook the noodles in it for about 6 to 8 minutes, until soft but still a little al dente. Remove the noodles with a skimmer, then blanch the spinach in this same pot of hot water for 1 minute. Transfer the cooked spinach to a bowl of ice water to help set their color. Set aside. Cut the cooked noodles into shorter lengths, roughly 5 inches long.

2. Mix the sauce by combining all the ingredients for it in a small bowl. Set this aside for later.

3. In a medium frying pan, heat the oil over medium heat. Sauté the carrot, shallots, scallions, and mushrooms together for around 5 minutes, until softened. Remove to a separate bowl, reserving the oil. Add the beef to the pan and cook for another 5 minutes, turning occasionally to make sure the meat is cooked. Move the cooked meat to the bowl with the vegetables and cover with the sauce.

4. Transfer the cooked noodles into the frying pan and cook for 1 minute or so, until they start to become a little sticky. Finally, add all the cooked vegetables, meat, and spinach back into the frying pan. Stir together for several minutes until the sauce is evenly dispersed. Add salt and pepper to taste. Serve hot, but it makes great leftovers.

"Is this easy mode?"

HOTTEOK

A popular street food, hotteok are delicious yeasted pancakes filled with a sweet mixture of brown sugar and crushed nuts. The chewy dough is complemented by the crunch of the nuts, and the whole thing makes for a special dessert.

Kids in South Korea enjoy these sweet treats every winter; they are just one small symbol of culture, tradition, and family—the very things that Hana and her best friend, Dae-hyun, are fighting every day to protect. And when victory is finally claimed, these beloved treats from home will definitely be on the menu.

ASIA · *D.Va*

TYPE: *CELEBRATORY*

HOTTEOK:

» ½ cup warm milk

» 1 teaspoon sugar

» 1 teaspoon instant yeast

» ½ teaspoon fine sea salt

» 1¼ cups all-purpose flour

» Cooking oil for frying

FILLING:

» ¼ cup packed dark brown sugar

» 1 teaspoon ground cinnamon

» 2 teaspoons honey

» 2 tablespoons crushed peanuts

PREP TIME: 25 minutes
RISING TIME: 1 hour
COOKING TIME: 15 minutes

YIELD: 6 pancakes

DIETARY: Vegetarian

1. Combine the milk, sugar, and yeast in a medium-size mixing bowl, stirring together to dissolve. Add the salt, and then gradually work in the flour until you have a nice smooth dough that isn't too sticky but is still soft. Cover with plastic wrap and let sit in a warm place for 1 hour, or until doubled in size. While the dough is rising, combine the ingredients for the filling in a small bowl and set aside.

2. Once the dough has risen, lightly oil your hands and divide the dough into 6 pieces. Working one at a time, form each piece of dough into a flat disc between your hands, and then spoon some of the filling onto the middle of it. Fold the sides of the dough over the filling and pinch together, enclosing the filling completely. Set each prepared dough packet aside while you finish the rest.

3. When all the dough has been prepped, heat a little cooking oil in a frying pan over medium heat. Place 1 or 2 of the dough balls, seam side down, in the hot pan, and press flat with an oiled spatula. Cook for about 30 seconds to 1 minute, until the underside is golden brown. Carefully flip the pancake and repeat on the other side. Remove to a plate lined with paper towels and repeat with the remaining dough balls.

"One for my highlight reel!"

CONGEE

Congee is often served as a simple but delightful savory breakfast, though it can also be eaten as a meal throughout the day. It's especially comforting in cold weather, which is why it was one of Mei's favorite dishes when she was working at Ecopoint: Antarctica. Mei used to double this recipe to feed her entire team, and though that thought evokes a bittersweet memory now, she still relishes the heartiness of this recipe and the great times she had with her teammates.

ASIA · *Mei*

TYPE: *COMFORT*

» 2 pounds chicken thighs, bone-in

» 6 cups water

» 2 tablespoons mirin

» ½ inch ginger, freshly grated, plus more for topping

» Pinch of salt

» ½ cup uncooked long-grain rice

» Sliced scallions, for topping

» Toasted sesame oil, for topping

 COOKING TIME: 2 hours

 YIELD: 2 to 4 servings

DIETARY: Gluten-Free

1. Add the chicken thighs and water to a medium saucepan over medium-high heat, and then cook at a simmer for about 30 minutes. Strain the broth into a clean bowl, reserving the meat. Pour the strained broth back into the pan, and add the mirin, ginger, salt, and rice. Turn the heat down to low and cover. Let this mixture cook for at least 1 hour, until the rice is cooked through and soft, like oatmeal. Check occasionally to see if you need to add a little more water.

2. When the meat on the chicken thighs has cooled, shred the meat and discard fat and bones. Add half the meat back to the cooking rice and reserve the other half for topping the bowls. When you're ready to serve, divide the rice mixture among serving bowls, add the reserved shredded chicken, and then top with freshly grated ginger, sliced scallions, and toasted sesame oil to taste.

"That's a-Mei-zing!"

ROUJIAMO PORK BUNS

Mei hails from Xi'an in China, which is home to a lush and unique culinary style that stems from its history as a crossroads of cultures as part of the Silk Road. These pork buns are a bit like a hamburger, strongly spiced and packed with tender braised meat. This dish is often paired with *liangpi* cold noodles, which make for a delicious hot-and-cold combination.

It was hard for Mei to get something like pork belly while stationed in Antarctica, but now that she's able to travel the world, she relishes the fact that she can make these more often.

ASIA • Mei

TYPE: COMFORT

FILLING:

- 1½ pounds pork belly, chopped into 2-inch pieces
- 2 stalks scallion, cut into 1-inch sections
- 1 teaspoon Chinese five-spice
- 1 bay leaf
- ¼ teaspoon chili powder
- 1½ tablespoons soy sauce
- 2 teaspoons Shaoxing rice wine
- 2 heaping tablespoons brown sugar
- 2 teaspoons cornstarch
- Parsley, to garnish

BUNS:

- 1 cup water
- 2 teaspoons sugar
- 1 tablespoon vegetable oil
- 2 teaspoons instant yeast
- 3 cups all-purpose flour

PREP TIME: 5 minutes
RISING TIME: 1 hour
COOKING TIME: 2 hours

YIELD: 6 buns

DIETARY: None

1. Combine the pork belly and the other ingredients for the filling except for the cornstarch in a medium saucepan. Add just enough water to cover the pork, and then bring to a boil. Reduce heat to a simmer, and let cook for about 1½ hours, or until the pork is soft.

2. While the pork is cooking, make the dough for the buns. Combine the water, sugar, oil, yeast, and just enough flour to bring the dough together into a kneadable consistency that isn't too sticky. Knead for several minutes, until soft and smooth. Put the dough in a clean bowl and cover with plastic wrap or a damp dish towel and move somewhere warm to rise for about 1 hour, or until doubled in size.

3. Once the dough has risen, deflate it and divide into 6 equal pieces. Working with one piece of dough at a time, roll it out into a rope about 8 inches long. Flatten the rope with a rolling pin, and then roll the flattened dough from one short end to the other into a tube shape. Stand the tube on one end, and flatten first with the palm of your hand, then with a rolling pin until it is roughly 4 to 5 inches across. Cook each disk of flattened dough in a dry frying pan over medium heat with the lid on, for around 1½ minutes on each side, until golden brown. Repeat with all the dough and set aside.

4. Once the pork is soft, remove it to a separate bowl. Using two forks, shred the pieces of pork belly, discarding any especially large pieces of fat. Return the shredded pork to the saucepan and cook for another 30 minutes. When done, stir together the cornstarch with a little cold water, and then pour this mixture into the saucepan to thicken the sauce. Remove the pork from the heat.

5. To serve, cut each of the buns most of the way through to form a top and a bottom. Spoon the filling into each bun, top with a little chopped parsley, and enjoy straightaway.

"Curiosity leads to new adventures!"

MANTOU BUNS

These easy buns are a terrific chaser to a spicy meal. Delicious either steamed or fried, the mantou are served dipped in condensed milk, which clings to the little buns and turns them into a sweet dessert.

Before taking up her post at Ecopoint: Antarctica, Mei always ordered mantou after finishing a meal at her favorite hot pot restaurant in Xi'an. She prefers the fried version, which has a little crunch to it.

ASIA • *Mei*

TYPE: *CELEBRATORY*

» ¾ cup warm water

» 2 tablespoons sugar

» Pinch of salt

» 1½ teaspoons instant yeast

» 2½ cups all-purpose flour, plus more for dusting

» 2 to 4 cups vegetable oil for frying

» ½ cup sweetened condensed milk, to serve

 PREP TIME: 10 minutes
RISING TIME: 1 hour
STEAMING TIME: 10 minutes per batch

 YIELD: About 24 bite-size buns

 DIETARY: Vegetarian

1. Combine the warm water, sugar, salt, and yeast in a medium-size mixing bowl. Gradually add the flour until you have a nice dough that isn't too sticky. Turn out onto a lightly floured work surface and knead for a couple of minutes, until the dough is smooth. Return to the bowl, cover, and let sit in a warm place for around 1 hour, or until the dough has doubled in size.

2. Once the dough has risen, bring a pot of water to a simmer with a steamer basket or strainer, lightly brushed with oil, set over it. Knead the dough again until smooth, and then divide into halves. Shape each half into a long log, roughly 1½ inches wide. Cut off the ends with a sharp knife, and then cut the log into pieces about 1 inch wide. Dust these lightly with flour, and then place in the steamer. Steam for around 10 minutes, until cooked through.

3. If you'd like to fry half of the mantou, warm several cups of vegetable oil over medium heat in a small saucepan. Working in batches, drop 3 to 4 mantou into the hot oil at a time, turning occasionally until they are browned all over. Remove from the oil and let drain on paper towels. Serve with condensed milk for dipping.

"We can do it together."

WINTER WARMER FIVE-SPICE HOT COCOA

Nothing can compare to a nice steaming mug of hot cocoa, especially in the winter when the land is covered in pristine blankets of snow. This beverage combines the richness of thick cocoa with an unexpected mix of spices to create a truly warming drink.

Mei developed this particular recipe while working in the frigid climate of Ecopoint: Antarctica and missing the flavors of home. The five-spice powder complemented the cocoa beautifully, and soon other members of her team began requesting it. She still thinks of them when she makes a batch.

ASIA · *Mei*

TYPE: *DRINK*

 PREP TIME: 5 minutes

YIELD: 2 servings

DIETARY: Gluten-F
Vegetarian

» ⅓ cup cocoa powder

» 2 to 3 tablespoons brown sugar, to taste

» 1 teaspoon Chinese five-spice powder

» 3 cups whole milk

» ¼ cup heavy cream

» Marshmallows or whipped cream, for topping

1. Begin by whisking the cocoa powder, br
   sugar, and Chinese five-spice powder
   together in a small bowl to make the h
   cocoa mix. Set aside.

2. Heat the milk over medium-low heat   ng
   frequently, until steam begins to sl
   rise from the surface and a couple   ll
   bubbles rise to the surface.

3. Whisk the hot cocoa mix into the
   thoroughly. Pour into two mugs a   with
   marshmallows or whipped crean

"I can't wait to get started."

BORSCHT

In the searing white coldness of Siberia, the shocking pink of this soup was a welcome burst of color that livened any table. Zarya enjoyed this soup often as a child, usually before training. Her mother would add eggs to the broth for extra protein. Whether Zarya's affection for this soup has anything to do with her hair color of choice is a matter for debate.

ASIA • *Zarya*

TYPE: *PREP*

PREP TIME: 15 minutes
COOKING TIME: 40 minutes

 YIELD: 4 servings

 DIETARY: Gluten-Free

- » 1 tablespoon unsalted butter
- » 1 large onion, diced
- » 4 cloves garlic, minced
- » 1 large carrot, diced
- » 1 pound beetroot, peeled and chopped into bite-size pieces
- » 6 cups chicken stock
- » 2 medium potatoes, peeled and diced
- » 1 teaspoon fresh dill, plus more for garnish
- » 1 teaspoon red wine vinegar
- » ¼ teaspoon sugar
- » Sour cream, to taste

1. Melt the butter in a large saucepot over medium heat, and then add the onion and garlic. Cook for several minutes, until fragrant and soft. Add the carrot, beetroot, and a splash of the stock, and then cover and cook for around 10 minutes.

2. Add the remaining stock, the potatoes, dill, vinegar, and sugar. Cook this mixture for around 30 minutes, or until the potatoes are soft. Scoop out about half of the cooked roots and place in a bowl temporarily.

3. Add a good dollop of sour cream to the pot, and then blend using an immersion blender (or in batches in a conventional blender). Add more sour cream to get the flavor and color you like, and then add the rest of the cooked vegetables back in. Ladle into serving bowls, garnish with extra dill and sour cream, and enjoy hot.

"Practice makes perfect."

PELMENI

These little dumplings feature deliciously savory meat covered by a thin dough wrapper. They can be boiled and served in soup or tossed with some melted butter and garnished with sour cream and fresh herbs like dill or parsley. Growing up in a remote Siberian village, Zarya loved these little pockets of meat and dough as a warm and welcome meal.

ASIA • *Zarya*

TYPE: *COMFORT*

PREP TIME: 15 minutes
SETTING TIME: 30 minutes
COOKING TIME: 40 minutes

YIELD: Enough for 4 large servings

DIETARY: None

DOUGH:

- » ¼ cup unsalted butter
- » 1 teaspoon salt
- » 3 cups all-purpose flour
- » 1 egg
- » 1 cup cold water

FILLING:

- » 1 medium yellow onion, diced
- » 4 cloves garlic
- » Small bunch parsley, with some reserved for garnish
- » Small bunch dill, with some reserved for garnish
- » 1 pound ground beef
- » 1 pound ground pork
- » Salt and pepper, to taste
- » 2 bay leaves for boiling
- » Sour cream, to serve

TO MAKE THE DOUGH:

1. In a large mixing bowl, rub together the butter, salt, and flour until there are no large pieces remaining. Add the egg, and then gradually mix in just enough water to pull the dough together without it being sticky. Turn out the dough onto a lightly floured surface and knead for a few minutes. Cover the dough and let sit at room temperature for around 30 minutes while you prepare the filling.

TO MAKE THE FILLING:

2. Run the onion, garlic, parsley, and dill through a food processor until minced fine. Transfer this mixture into a large mixing bowl along with the ground meats and salt and pepper to taste. Mix until everything is evenly distributed.

3. Divide the dough into 4 equal pieces and cover three to keep them from drying out. Roll the remaining quarter of dough out on a lightly floured surface very thin, to about ⅛ inch.

4. Using a round cutter, cut dough into discs about 2 to 3 inches across. Place a dollop of filling, roughly 2 teaspoons' worth, on half of a disc, avoiding the outside edges. Fold the dough in half, pressing with your fingertips to seal the edges together in a half-moon shape. Then take the corners and fold them away from the curved edge, pinching them together to make your final shape. Repeat with the remaining dough and filling.

5. To cook, bring a large pot of water to boil with the bay leaves for extra seasoning. Working a batch at a time, drop several handfuls of pelmeni into the boiling water. Stir to make sure they don't stick to the bottom, and then cook for 5 to 10 minutes. The dumplings should float to the top of the water when they are done. Remove from water and serve warm, topped with sour cream and a sprinkle of the reserved dill and parsley.

TIP: The uncooked pelmeni freeze well if you do not need the entire batch. Just toss with a little extra flour to keep them from sticking to one another, and put in a freezer bag.

"Get down! Give me twenty."

RUSSIAN HONEY CAKE

Although the specific ingredients and techniques used to make this cake vary wildly, this particular recipe is one that Zarya enjoys when she wants to celebrate.

What begins as a stack of almost-cookies softens over time with the help of layers of icing. The taste is reminiscent of a graham cracker, with the cooked honey flavor vying with the sweetened sour cream icing.

ASIA • *Zarya*

TYPE: *CELEBRATORY*

 PREP TIME: 20 minutes
BAKING TIME: 20 minutes
CHILLING TIME: 8 hours or overnight

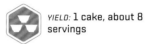 YIELD: 1 cake, about 8 servings

 DIETARY: Vegetarian

CAKE:

» 4 tablespoons unsalted butter

» ¾ cup granulated sugar

» 4 tablespoons honey

» 3 eggs, beaten

» 1 teaspoon baking soda

» 3 cups all-purpose flour

ICING:

» 1 cup heavy cream

» 1 cup powdered sugar

» 16 ounces sour cream

TO MAKE THE CAKE:

1. Preheat oven to 350°F and line a baking sheet with parchment paper. Melt the butter in a medium saucepan over medium-low heat, and then add the sugar to it, stirring to combine. In a separate bowl, whisk together the honey, eggs, and baking soda. Add this mixture to the saucepan, continuing to whisk while doing so. Continue to stir the mixture over medium-low heat, scraping the bottom to keep it from burning. After around 10 minutes, the mixture should have puffed up and darkened to a deep golden color. Remove from heat.

2. Gradually stir in the flour, transferring the dough to a clean work surface when it begins to grow too difficult to mix in the pan. Knead a few times until you have a dough that is not sticky but is soft and pliable. Divide the dough into 8 equal pieces. Then, working one at a time, roll out the dough on a lightly floured surface as thin as possible. Cut into an 8-to-9-inch circle, using a pan or a pot lid as a template and tracing with a knife, saving the scraps of dough.

3. Place 2 of these discs at a time on the prepared baking sheet and bake for 4 to 5 minutes, until puffed a little and darker brown. Remove to a cooling rack to cool completely and repeat with the remaining dough. Combine and reroll the dough scraps to create additional layers.

TO MAKE THE ICING:

4. While the cake layers are cooling, whip the heavy cream to stiff peaks, and then quickly beat in the powdered sugar. Fold in the sour cream.

5. When you are ready to assemble the cake, place 1 disc of cooked dough on your serving dish. Add a dollop of the icing on top and spread it around evenly. Add another cookie disc on top of this, and then continue layering the icing and cake layers. Finish the cake by icing the top and sides, and then allow the cake to sit in the fridge overnight, or at least 8 hours, to soften.

6. While the cake chills, pulse the baked scraps in a food processor until you have a nice even crumb texture. Once the cake is chilled, gently press this crumb mixture to the top and sides. Serve alongside strong tea or coffee.

"Savor this victory."

SUPER NOVA

This drink became all the rage in St. Petersburg after an enterprising bartender created the drink and named it after Russia's protector, Aleksandra Zaryanova. Some might confuse this cocktail for a lightweight's beverage of choice, but be warned: This pink drink punches above its weight class. A symbol of resilience and excellence, Zarya doesn't settle for weakness, and neither does her drink of choice.

This pink twist on a White Russian is all you need to get on her level and meet the next challenge.

ASIA · *Zarya*

TYPE: *DRINK*

 PREP TIME: 5 minutes

 YIELD: 1 serving

 DIETARY: Gluten-Free, Vegetarian

» 3 ounces heavy cream

» 2 ounces Absolut Raspberri

» ½ ounce grenadine or more to taste

1. Combine all the ingredients in a cocktail shaker half filled with ice and shake vigorously for a few seconds. Pour over ice into a rocks glass and serve immediately.

"From Russia with love."

PAKORA

These snackable fritters are commonly found throughout India. Symmetra first encountered these delicious bites as a small child at one of these bustling food stalls near her home in Hyderabad. Though Utopaea does not have anything as free-form as food stalls lining its streets, Symmetra still appreciates when she can get a plate of crisp pakoras served with a little bit of chutney or raita.

ASIA • *Symmetra*

TYPE: *PREP*

PREP TIME: 5 minutes
FRYING TIME: 20 minutes

YIELD: About 12 pakora

DIETARY: Gluten-Free, Vegan

› Vegetable oil for frying
› ½ medium yellow onion, sliced thin
› 2 cups cauliflower florets
› 1 potato, cubed small
› 2 cloves garlic, minced
› 2 tablespoons minced cilantro
› 1 teaspoon curry powder
› ½ teaspoon salt
› Pinch of cayenne pepper
› 1½ cups chickpea flour
› ¾ to 1 cup cold water

1. Add about 2 inches of vegetable oil to the bottom of a medium saucepan and set over medium heat until it reaches around 350°F. Combine the onion, cauliflower, potato, and garlic in a large mixing bowl. Toss with the seasonings, and then set aside.

2. In a separate bowl, combine the chickpea flour and just enough of the water to make a batter that is relatively thick and smooth but will still run off a spoon. Pour this over the vegetables and toss to cover evenly.

3. To fry, drop portions of the batter, about ½ cup at a time, into the hot oil. Let each of the pakora cook for about 1 minute, and then flip over and cook on the other side. They should be a beautiful golden brown and a little crispy when done.

"If I can think it, I can create it."

CHICKEN CURRY

Growing up, Symmetra lived in a crowded and chaotic place that disturbed her orderly mind. When she was whisked away to Vishkar's Architech Academy, she found solace in the structured world of Utopaea. Occasionally, in a quiet moment, she'll put together a pot of this chicken curry, made with flavors she remembers from home. The rich flavor of this simple dish from her childhood is worlds apart from the fancy food at the academy, but Symmetra still appreciates the deep, comforting flavors.

ASIA • Symmetra

TYPE: COMFORT

PREP TIME: 5 minutes
COOKING TIME: 35 minutes

 YIELD: 4 servings

 DIETARY: Gluten-Free

» 3 tablespoons vegetable oil

» 1 teaspoon ground cardamom

» 1 teaspoon ground cinnamon

» 1 teaspoon curry powder

» ¼ teaspoon ground cloves

» 1 medium yellow onion, diced

» 1 pound chicken drumsticks, skin removed

» 2 inches ginger, freshly grated

» 6 cloves garlic, minced

» 1 teaspoon mild chili powder

» Pinch of turmeric powder

» 2 bay leaves

» 2 tablespoons Greek yogurt

› ¼ cup water

› Salt, to taste

› Coriander or parsley for garnish

1. Pour the vegetable oil into a large frying pan over medium heat. Add the cardamom, cinnamon, curry powder, and cloves, stirring for around 1 minute, until fragrant.

2. Add the onion and cook for several minutes, until softened. Next, add the chicken, ginger, and garlic and cook for several more minutes, turning the chicken occasionally. Add the remaining ingredients and salt to taste. Cover the pan, and let simmer for around 20 minutes.

3. To serve, divide the drumsticks between serving bowls and pour the sauce over each. Garnish with coriander or parsley. This curry is great spooned over rice.

"I will shape order from chaos."

KAJU KATLI

This simple fudge-like dessert made from cashew flour and ghee (clarified butter) is packed with delicious, melt-in-your-mouth flavor. Symmetra takes great pleasure in making this dish because, though the recipe itself is simple, she can cut the fudge into precise geometric shapes and create a pristine display.

ASIA • *Symmetra*

TYPE: *CELEBRATORY*

» ½ cup sugar

» ¼ cup water

» 1 cup cashew flour

» 1 tablespoon ghee

» Pinch of ground cardamom

» Edible silver leaf (optional)

PREP TIME: 15 minutes
DRYING TIME: 20 minutes

YIELD: Around 20 pieces

DIETARY: Gluten-Free, Vegetarian

1. Cut out and butter a piece of parchment paper at least 12 inches square and set nearby.

2. Combine the sugar and water in a small saucepan over medium heat. Cook for a few minutes, stirring occasionally, until the sugar has dissolved. Once the sugar has thickened somewhat and is bubbling, add the cashew flour. Stir for a few minutes more, until the whole mixture starts to ball up in the pan, rather than separating. Remove from heat and add the ghee and cardamom.

3. Turn this out onto the buttered parchment paper and spread out slightly to help cool. Once the fudge is cool enough to touch, knead several times until it's a smooth consistency. Using a lightly buttered rolling pin, roll out to between ½ inch and ¼ inch thick.

4. If using the silver leaf, gently lay it on the rolled-out fudge, pressing it down onto the sticky surface. Then, using a sharp buttered knife, cut the fudge into diamond shapes. Let these dry for around 20 minutes, and then arrange in a geometrical pattern to serve.

TIP: Edible silver leaf can be applied to the top of the fudge before slicing to give the Kaju Katli an especially stunning shine.

"Beauty can be found where everything is in harmony."

HYDERABADI LASSI

A traditional summertime drink in India, a lassi is a thick yogurt-based beverage, almost dessert-like in texture and flavor. It can be made in many different flavors, but in Symmetra's hometown of Hyderabad, the most common variety is Rooh Afza, a rose-scented syrup that gives this drink its distinctive color and flavor. Symmetra wasn't able to get her hands on this drink too often growing up. Now, she'll mix one together on occasion and remember that special treats from childhood can still be savored.

ASIA • *Symmetra*

TYPE: *DRINK*

 PREP TIME: 5 minutes

 YIELD: 2 small servings or 1 large

 DIETARY: Gluten-Free, Vegetarian

» 2 cups plain yogurt
» ½ cup cold water
» ½ cup sugar
» 1 to 2 tablespoons Rooh Afza syrup or other flavored syrup
» Vanilla ice cream, for topping (optional)
» Edible flowers, for topping (optional)
» Crushed pistachios, for topping (optional)

1. In a medium-size mixing bowl, beat together the yogurt, water, and sugar until smooth.

2. Add the Rooh Afza syrup and beat again until it is completely combined.

3. Pour the mixture into serving glasses, and top with your desired toppings. Enjoy immediately.

"A performance worthy of repetition."

TIL KO LADDU SESAME SWEETS

These simple little round sweets burst with the earthiness of sesame seeds and the rich flavor of raw sugar. With a texture halfway between chewy and crumbly, they are sure to win over cynics and bring peace to conflict.

Despite being unable to eat, Zenyatta knows to use food to help spread empathy and peace to those they encounter. These "orbs" probably won't heal a friend or hinder an enemy, but you can always try.

ASIA • *Zenyatta*

TYPE: *PREP*

» 1 cup sesame seeds

» 1 cup jaggery sugar, or ¾ cup packed light brown sugar

» 2 tablespoons ghee or regular unsalted butter

» ½ cup whole milk

 COOKING TIME: 10 minutes

 YIELD: 12 balls

 DIETARY: Gluten-Free, Vegetarian

1. Lightly butter a small bowl and set aside. Place the sesame seeds in a medium frying pan over medium heat and begin to roast them, swirling or stirring constantly, until they are toasted and just starting to smell fragrant.

2. Add the remaining ingredients and cook, stirring occasionally, until the mixture has thickened somewhat and is beginning to bubble. Remove from heat and pour into the buttered bowl.

3. After several minutes, when the mixture has begun to cool enough to handle, lightly butter your hands and form into a dozen bite-size balls. Place these on a clean plate to finish cooling.

"Consider only victory. Make defeat an impossibility in your mind."

MOMOS

With the sharp bite of spices and a soft, pillowy bun, these dumplings are truly little orbs of delight. Traditionally, this Tibetan dish features meat fillings, but Zenyatta prefers to share a vegan version with those he has met during his travels—Genji included.

ASIA • Zenyatta

TYPE: **COMFORT**

PREP TIME: 20 minutes
RISING TIME: 1 hour
STEAMING TIME: 15 to 20 minutes

YIELD: 8 dumplings

DIETARY: Vegan

BUNS:

- » ½ cup warm water
- » 1 tablespoon vegetable oil
- » 4 teaspoons to 3 tablespoons sugar
- » ½ teaspoon fine sea salt
- » 2 teaspoon instant yeast
- » 2½ cups all-purpose flour

FILLING:

- » 2 tablespoons vegetable oil for frying
- » 1 tablespoon freshly grated ginger
- » 1 tablespoon minced garlic
- » ½ small yellow onion, diced
- » 2 tablespoons tomato paste
- » Splash of toasted sesame oil
- » ½ teaspoon turmeric
- » ½ teaspoon cumin
- » ¼ teaspoon red pepper flakes
- » Salt and pepper, to taste
- » 10 ounces button mushrooms
- » 1 cup fresh or frozen peas, thawed
- » 2 teaspoons cornstarch

TO MAKE THE BUN DOUGH:

1. In a medium-size mixing bowl, combine the warm water, oil, sugar, salt, and yeast. Gradually add the flour, about ½ cup at a time, until you have a dough that is not sticky and can be kneaded. Turn out onto a lightly floured surface and knead for several minutes, adding a little more flour as needed, until soft and pillowy. Place back in a clean bowl, cover with a damp towel or plastic, and set in a warm place to rise for about 1 hour, or until doubled in size.

TO MAKE THE FILLING:

2. While the dough is rising, start your filling mixture so it has a chance to cool before you shape the dumplings. Heat the oil in a frying pan over medium heat. Add the ginger and garlic and cook for several minutes, until soft and just turning golden brown. Add the onion and cook for a few more minutes until soft. Add the tomato paste, the splash of sesame oil, the spices, and some salt and pepper to taste.

3. Cook this mixture for several minutes, until fragrant. Finally, add the mushrooms, stirring to make sure they are evenly coated with the spice mixture. Let this cook together for around 5 minutes, until the mushrooms are soft and evenly mixed with everything else.

4. Remove from the heat and stir in the peas. In a small bowl or cup, mix the cornstarch with just enough water to dissolve it. Stir this solution into the mushroom pan to help thicken the filling a little.

» Continued on page 202...

"Repetition is the path to mastery."

TO ASSEMBLE:

5. Once your dough has risen, divide it into 8 equal pieces. Roll each piece into a ball, and then flatten to a disc about 4 inches across, flattening the outermost edges a little more. When the filling is cool, divide that into 8 equal portions as well. Holding a circle of dough flat in one hand, add a scoop of the filling to the middle of it. Starting at one edge, gather the dough into a little fold, pressing between your fingertips. From there, continue adding accordion folds as you work your way around the dumpling, turning as you go, until you run out of space. Pinch the last bit closed and give the whole dumpling a little twist to line up the diagonal pleats.

6. Place the filled dumplings on small squares of parchment paper and arrange in your steamer. Steam for around 15 to 20 minutes, then take off the heat and let sit for another 5 minutes or so, covered. Best enjoyed the same day.

TIBETAN BUTTER TEA

A steaming bowl of this tea is the first thing given to the human pilgrims who make the arduous trek up the mountains to Shambali Monastery. Its flavors may surprise the travelers at first, but once the savory, creamy tea passes their lips, they'll find that this salt-and-butter drink promotes restoration and provides sustenance and inner harmony.

ASIA • *Zenyatta*

TYPE: *DRINK*

 PREP TIME: 5 minutes

 YIELD: 2 servings

 DIETARY: Gluten-Free, Vegetarian

» 4 cups boiling water
» 2 black tea bags
» ¼ teaspoon salt
» 2 tablespoons unsalted butter
» ⅓ cup heavy cream

1. Steep the two tea bags in the boiling water for several minutes, until you have the strength of tea you like. When the tea is ready, stir in the salt until dissolved, and then add the butter and cream.

2. At this point, the tea is traditionally worked into a froth in a tall churn, but an immersion blender also works. In a pinch, it can also be shaken vigorously in a sealed jar. Churn, blend, or shake for at least a minute, until frothy, and then divide equally between two cups. Serve hot.

"True self is without form."

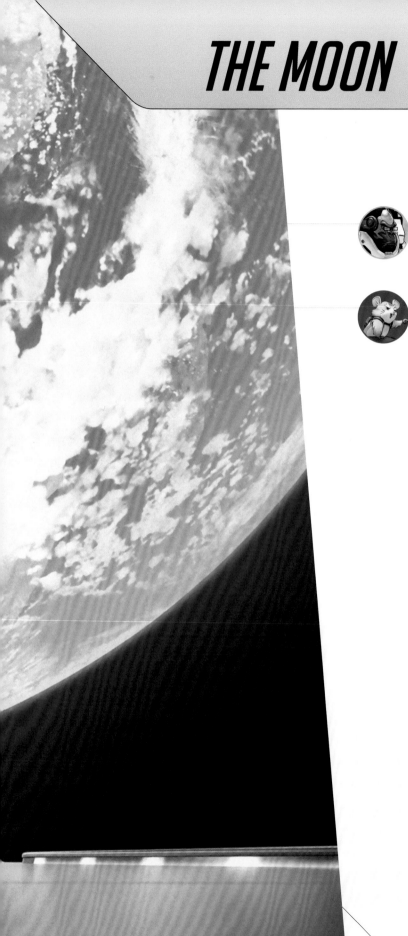

THE MOON

PINEAPPLE PIZZA

While this particular pizza-topping combination can be divisive, it became one of Winston's favorites. It was always in the center of the table, whether on the Orca or back at one of the Watchpoints, and slices were passed around and enjoyed amid much laughter. Winston took a little convincing at first, but he has very fond memories of sharing this meal with his team and his friends.

THE MOON · *Winston*

TYPE: **CELEBRATORY**

DOUGH:

- » 1 cup water
- » 1 tablespoon sugar
- » 2 teaspoons active dry yeast
- » 3 tablespoons olive oil, plus more for brushing
- » 1½ teaspoons salt
- » 3½ cups all-purpose flour, plus more for dusting

TOPPINGS:

- » ½ cup tomato pizza sauce, or more to taste
- » 1½ cups shredded mozzarella cheese
- » ½ cup cooked ham or Canadian bacon, sliced or chopped
- » ½ cup pineapple chunks (canned or fresh)
- » 3 slices bacon, cooked and crumbled
- » A few slices red onion

PREP TIME: 5 minutes
RISING TIME: 1 hour
BAKING TIME: 15 minutes

YIELD: 1 pizza, 8 servings

DIETARY: None

TO MAKE THE DOUGH:

1. In a medium-size mixing bowl, combine the water, sugar, yeast, oil, and salt. Gradually add the flour until you have a dough that isn't too sticky to be handled. Sprinkle a little extra flour on a clean work surface and knead the dough for a couple of minutes, until soft and pliable. Return to the bowl, cover with plastic, and set in a warm place for about 1 hour, or until doubled in size.

TO ASSEMBLE:

2. Once the dough is ready, preheat the oven to 450°F and line a large baking sheet with parchment paper. Press the dough into a flat disc roughly 20 inches across with lightly oiled fingers, leaving the edges of the pizza a little thicker for the crust, about a half-inch to an inch wide. Spread the sauce over the dough, sprinkle with cheese, and top with the ham, pineapple, crumbled bacon, and red onion. Bake for about 15 minutes, until golden and cooked through. Slice and serve!

LUNAR OPS

"Natural selection!"

HORIZON LUNAR COLONY PIES

They say you can never go home again—but sometimes you can bring a little piece of home with you. Winston has fond memories of living on the moon, and his time at the Horizon Lunar Colony made him who he is today. Dr. Harold Winston used to make these gooey marshmallow, cookie, and chocolate treats popularized in the US South for his fellow scientists to mark special occasions.

THE MOON • *Winston*

TYPE: *CELEBRATORY*

PREP TIME: 20 minutes
BAKING TIME: 20 minutes
CHILLING TIME: 30 minutes

YIELD: 8 to 10 moon pies

DIETARY: Vegetarian

- » 6 tablespoons unsalted butter, softened
- » ½ cup packed dark brown sugar
- » ½ teaspoon vanilla extract
- » 1 large egg
- » 1½ cups graham cracker crumbs (about 8 crackers)
- » ½ teaspoon baking powder
- » ½ teaspoon baking soda
- » A pinch of salt
- » ¾ cup all-purpose flour
- » 1½ cups marshmallow fluff
- » 10 ounces chocolate chips
- » 1 tablespoon vegetable oil

1. Preheat the oven to 350°F and line a baking sheet with parchment paper.

2. In a large mixing bowl, cream together the butter and brown sugar until smooth. Add the vanilla and egg, followed by the graham cracker crumbs, baking powder, baking soda, and salt. Finally, add the flour and mix thoroughly, until you have a dough that isn't too sticky.

3. Divide the dough in half, and then roll one half out on a lightly floured surface to about ¼ inch thick. Using a 3-inch round cookie cutter or a glass, cut out as many cookie discs as you can from the dough.

4. Arrange the cookies on the prepared baking sheet and bake for about 10 minutes. Let sit on the hot baking sheet for a minute or two, and then transfer the cookies to a wire rack to cool completely. Repeat with the remaining dough, rerolling the scraps as well.

5. Once the cookies are completely cool, add a dollop of about 2 tablespoons marshmallow fluff to the center of half of them. Place another cookie on top of the fluff and gently press the cookies together to evenly distribute the fluff between them. Repeat with all the cookies, and then place the sandwiches in the freezer to chill while you prepare the chocolate coating.

6. Melt the chocolate chips either in a double boiler over the stove or in short bursts in the microwave, stirring occasionally until you have a smooth consistency. Stir in the vegetable oil.

7. Take the cookie sandwiches out of the freezer, and working one at a time, balance a sandwich on a spatula or fork over the bowl of chocolate. Using a large spoon, coat the top of the sandwich, letting the chocolate run over the sides. Smooth out any bare spots, and then place on a wire rack to set. The cold cookies should help the chocolate set much quicker than usual. Repeat with the remaining cookies, and then chill in the fridge until ready to serve.

"No, I do not want a banana."

PEANUT BUTTER PUDDING

Although most of us would eat this pudding with a spoon, Winston uses it as a dip for bananas, allowing him to enjoy his favorite food (peanut butter) and tolerate his least favorite (bananas) while keeping an eye on global affairs.

THE MOON • *Winston*

TYPE: **COMFORT**

 COOKING TIME: 10 minutes

 YIELD: 4 servings

 DIETARY: Gluten-Free, Vegetarian

» ¼ cup sugar
» Pinch of salt
» ⅓ cup cornstarch
» 3 cups whole milk
» ¼ cup honey
» 1½ cups peanut butter
» 2 teaspoons vanilla extract
» ½ teaspoons ground cinnamon
» 2 sliced bananas, for topping
» Whipped cream, for topping

1. Whisk together the sugar, salt, and cornstarch in a medium saucepan. Add the milk and honey and cook this mixture over medium heat, whisking occasionally. Bring to a simmer, at which point the whole mix should thicken noticeably.

2. Remove from heat and stir in the peanut butter, vanilla, and cinnamon. Allow the pudding to cool for a few minutes, and then divide into serving dishes. Top with slices of bananas and a dollop of whipped cream.

TIP: The pudding can also be covered with plastic wrap and chilled for several days in the fridge.

"Did someone say peanut butter?"

HAMSTER FOOD

Hammond put together his battle mech by patching scrap metal and other materials lying around Junkertown onto his lunar escape pod. In the same way, this recipe is a mishmash of various ingredients that come together in one crispy, crunchy, nutty treat that can sate any appetite, even in the apocalyptic wastes.

THE MOON • *Wrecking Ball*

TYPE: *PREP*

 PREP TIME: 10 minutes
CHILLING TIME: 1 hour

 YIELD: About 12 bars

 DIETARY: Vegetarian

» 1 cup puffed rice cereal

» 1 cup Lúcio-Oh's, or similar cereal

» ½ teaspoons ground cinnamon

» ½ cup sunflower seeds

» ½ cup pumpkin seeds

» ¼ cup rolled oats

» ½ cup chocolate chips or other chocolate candy

» ½ cup cranberries, raisins, or other dried fruit

» ½ cup peanut butter

» ½ cup honey

» ¼ cup packed light brown sugar

1. In a medium-size bowl, combine all dry ingredients and mix together until well combined. Lightly butter a square 9-by-9-inch baking pan and set aside.

2. Melt together the peanut butter, honey, and brown sugar either in the microwave or in a small saucepan until runny. Pour this mixture over the dry ingredients, while stirring, until everything is equally covered. Transfer everything into the prepared baking pan, pressing flat. Let chill for at least 1 hour, and then cut into snack-size pieces.

Angry Squeaking

CHEESE WRECKING BALL

Hammond thinks this tasty snack is the spitting image of his battle mech, and the much-loved flavor combination of an everything bagel with savory cheese makes this cheese ball an arena champion.

THE MOON • *Wrecking Ball*

TYPE: *CELEBRATORY*

PREP TIME: 10 minutes
CHILLING TIME: 1 hour

YIELD: 1 cheese ball

DIETARY: Gluten-Free, Vegetarian

› 8 ounces cream cheese, softened

› 8 ounces white cheddar, grated

› 2 teaspoons dried minced onion, divided

› 2 teaspoons dried minced garlic, divided

› 2 teaspoons toasted sesame seeds

› 2 teaspoons poppy seeds

1. In a food processor, combine the cream cheese, cheddar, and half the onion and garlic. Pulse several times, until the whole mixture starts to ball up in the machine; you can also blend everything by hand in a mixing bowl. Using damp hands, form into a ball shape, and then wrap in plastic and chill for 1 hour.

2. While the cheese ball is chilling, mix together the sesame seeds, poppy seeds, and the rest of the garlic and onion in a shallow bowl. When the cheese is ready, unwrap it and roll in the topping mixture until completely covered. Serve at room temperature with plenty of crackers.

"The hamster is pleased."

INSIGHT EDITIONS

PO Box 3088
San Rafael, CA 94912
www.insighteditions.com

Find us on Facebook: www.facebook.com/InsightEditions
Follow us on Twitter: @insighteditions

Library of Congress Cataloging-in-Publication Data available.

ISBN: 978-1-68383-588-2

Publisher: Raoul Goff
President: Kate Jerome
Associate Publisher: Vanessa Lopez
Creative Director: Chrissy Kwasnik
Designer: Evelyn Furuta
Managing Editor: Lauren LePera
Senior Editor: Amanda Ng
Editorial Assistant: Maya Alpert
Production Editors: Jennifer Bentham and Elaine Ou
Senior Production Manager: Greg Steffen

Insight Editions would like to thank Anna Eames for her editorial contributions to this book.

ROOTS of PEACE   REPLANTED PAPER

Insight Editions, in association with Roots of Peace, will plant two trees for each tree used in the manufacturing of this book. Roots of Peace is an internationally renowned humanitarian organization dedicated to eradicating land mines worldwide and converting war-torn lands into productive farms and wildlife habitats. Roots of Peace will plant two million fruit and nut trees in Afghanistan and provide farmers there with the skills and support necessary for sustainable land use.

Manufactured in China by Insight Editions

10 9 8 7 6 5 4 3 2 1

ABOUT THE AUTHOR

Chelsea Monroe-Cassel is the coauthor of the best seller *A Feast of Ice and Fire: The Official Game of Thrones Companion Cookbook* and the author of *World of Warcraft: The Official Cookbook*, *Hearthstone: Innkeeper's Tavern Cookbook*, and *The Elder Scrolls: The Official Cookbook*. Her work is a synthesis of imagination and historical research. This passion has led her to a career of transforming imaginary foods into reality. She greatly enjoys foreign languages, treasure hunting, history, and all things related to honey.

BLIZZARD ENTERTAINMENT

Editors: Allison Irons, Paul Morrissey
Creative Consultation: Michael Chu, Arnold Tsang
Lore Consultation: Sean Copeland, Christi Kugler, Justin Parker
Production: Phillip Hilldenbrand, Brianne M Loftis, Alix Nicholaeff, Derek Rosenberg, Jeffrey Wong
Director, Consumer Products: Byron Parnell
Directors, Creative Development: Ralph Sanchez, David Seeholzer